THE
COURAGE
TO BE
IMPERFECT

How to Release Yourself from Unrealistic
Expectations and START ENJOYING LIFE

ELIZABETH DANKS ROBBINS

BakerBooks

a division of Baker Publishing Group
Grand Rapids, Michigan

Published by Baker Books
a division of Baker Publishing Group
Grand Rapids, Michigan
BakerBooks.com

Printed in the United States of America

Library of Congress Cataloging-in-Publication Data
Names: Robbins, Elizabeth Danks, 1990– author.
Title: The courage to be imperfect : how to release yourself from unrealistic expectations and start enjoying life / Elizabeth Danks Robbins.
Description: Grand Rapids, Michigan : Baker Books, a division of Baker Publishing Group, [2025]
Identifiers: LCCN 2024033536 | ISBN 9781540904454 (paper) | ISBN 9781540904935 (casebound) | ISBN 9781493450404 (ebook)
Subjects: LCSH: Self-actualization (Psychology) | Self-realization in women. | Imperfection.
Classification: LCC BF637.S4 R5756 2025 | DDC 158.1—dc23/eng/20241231
LC record available at https://lccn.loc.gov/2024033536

25   26   27   28   29   30   31   7   6   5   4   3   2   1

For my sister, Emily.
Enjoy life, don't perfect it.

CONTENTS

INTRODUCTION

We Are Not Called to Be Perfect

I was sixteen, standing in the bread aisle at the grocery store, the first time a stranger walked up to me and told me I was throwing my life away. I was buying bread, and I was pregnant. Something about that made her decide she should tell me how she felt about it.

Unfortunately, she wasn't the only person to share her opinion with me. Hearing comments like "You are going to give that baby up for adoption, right?" and "Babies shouldn't raise babies" became routine for me, not only during my pregnancy but for years as a teen mom. Everywhere I turned, people expected me to fail. I didn't have to assume they were judging me. The polite ones whispered. The inconsiderate ones said their rude comments straight to my face. The inability to go into any public place without being shamed was a heavy weight for me to carry as an adolescent already struggling with confidence and self-worth. I felt like I was being crushed under a giant pile of opinions. I was fearful that all those watching eyes would catch any little mistake I made and I would be forced to give up my baby. There was nowhere I could go that pregnant teenagers were accepted. There was no one telling me I could do it, and it was the loneliest time of my life.

The Day My Perfectionism Started

I was sitting on my bathroom floor waiting for my pregnancy test results. It didn't take the full three minutes the box said it would. It felt like only seconds had passed when the test turned positive. And the moment it did, my life stopped being about me. It was like a switch flipped inside me. I became a mother right there on the bathroom floor.

I started planning and preparing. I had to figure out how I was going to do this. How was I going to support us? How was I going to tell my mother? How would I handle being up all night with a baby while going to school? I put all my efforts into figuring out how to pivot and make this work. But I didn't think about or prepare for the expectations other people would have for me and how they would tear me apart for the next decade.

I don't know if I can accurately describe loving your child, wanting nothing more than to raise him, and feeling like the world is watching and waiting for any excuse not to let you. Maybe you've felt that too. Maybe you've felt the pressure of trying to prove someone wrong about you. Every day, I felt immense pressure to prove to the world that I could take care of my baby. I felt like I had to prove I deserved the chance to be a mother.

So I tried to prove myself. I worked as hard as I could. I dropped out of high school and got my GED. At seventeen, I decided to go to nursing school so I would have a stable career that would support us. For the next four years, I applied for daycare assistance, tuition assistance, and student loans so I could afford diapers and food. I told myself that I had to get my bachelor's degree in four years. I thought that would really prove something to everyone, to all those people who thought I was throwing my life away.

My life revolved around daycare drop-offs, school, evenings with my son, and nights doing homework. I didn't really want to be a nurse, but I had to do something because I needed to survive, and I felt like I needed to prove myself as a worthy mom. *If I can do all of this, maybe they will respect me. Maybe they will stop telling me I can't do it. Maybe I'll feel worthy enough to be his mom.* I felt trapped underneath the immense pressure to be perfect and never fail. It was crushing me and made my life so much more complicated than it ever should have been.

But why? Why did I feel like I *had* to do all of this?

I lived under the pressure of perfectionism for years. I was trying to do everything right, fearing one mistake would lead my life off track and someone would say, "See? She can't do it." The opinions of strangers weighed heavy, but it was the opinions of people I loved that hurt the most.

My family members looked at me like I had died. One even told me, "You aren't going to hang around this town and go to school pregnant." I was called a slut and constantly criticized by people who had always told me they loved me.

I was a straight A student who worked two jobs. But overnight, I had lost the respect of the adults in my life. This was a hard fall. I was lonely, stressed, and offended. I was offended that the people who had trusted me to babysit their children just days before suddenly lost all faith in my abilities. The people who told me I could do anything I set my mind to were now telling me I couldn't do it.

I thought I needed to prove to them that I could still do anything I set my mind to. So I graduated in four years, met my husband, married him, bought a house, had another baby, and worked full-time as a pediatric emergency room nurse. That's when things started changing.

People stopped judging me for being a teen mom and started praising me for what I had accomplished. When someone would ask me if my kids were my little brothers, I had ammunition ready. No, I would say. Then I would throw my story at them. I would tell them I was married and that I was a nurse. Looks of judgment would transform into looks of amazement. After years of criticism, praise felt *good*. I started linking my worth to my achievements. I started building myself up on the approval of others. The main focus of my life was based on other people's opinions.

I loved my life. I loved my husband and my kids. But it all still felt really hard. On the outside, I was successful. On the inside, I was overwhelmed and felt like I needed an escape. Trying to keep up with work, kids, and a home, all while worrying about everyone's opinion of my life, had left me defeated. Every night, I would sit on my couch looking at the piles of laundry and sink full of dishes and wonder why I couldn't seem to keep up.

I felt like I was drowning in my to-do list. I was behind before I even got out of bed in the morning. I could never live up to the kind of wife, mother, and person I wanted to be. The kind I expected myself to be. That perfect version of myself I had envisioned. That perfect person I always fell short of.

I wouldn't have dared to call myself a perfectionist at the time. I pictured a perfectionist as a well-dressed lady with curled hair, who was obsessed with scrubbing her floors and organizing her closet by color. That wasn't me. My floors were sticky, and my closet floor was covered with dirty clothes. I wasn't perfect enough to be a perfectionist.

But who is a perfectionist? I wasn't trying to be the most stylish, the smartest, or the best at everything, but I was trying to live up to the expectations I believed in. A *perfectionist* isn't necessarily *perfect*. If you are trying to control your surroundings to meet an expectation that you have created in your head, that is your own version of perfection. If you feel bad about yourself when you can't live up to those expectations, that could be perfectionism.

Perfectionism can show up in a thousand different ways. It can look like a messy house because when you don't have time to clean the kitchen perfectly, you don't clean it at all. It can look like weeks of eating out because every time you try to cook, it doesn't turn out right, and you don't want to fail at something again. Perfectionism can prevent you from signing up for something you are interested in because you don't want to be the oldest or youngest person in the class. It can stop you from trying something new because you don't want to fail in front of people. Perfectionism is a problem when it starts to control your life and prevents you from enjoying it.

More times than I would like to admit, I have wanted to escape my life because I felt overwhelmed by the mess or the to-do list. It takes too much energy to be that perfect person living in the perfect house, and I felt completely drained. I was constantly searching for information to help me get my life together. I read all the self-help books. I watched all the motivational TED Talks and YouTube videos. I tried every cleaning method and routine I could find to help me get into a rhythm of staying on top of housework. Then I would find something—some little nugget of information, some magical cleaning tip, some parenting wisdom—and I would cling to it.

I would be overjoyed with the fact that I just figured out life, and I would be motivated by my new life hack for about a week. And then something would ruin my momentum. A kid would get sick, or I would get home too late to do my evening cleaning routine. Something would throw me off, and I would end up leaving the dishes in the sink. The laundry would pile up again, and I would forget to take a kid to soccer practice. I *was* a perfectionist—if I couldn't do it perfectly, I just didn't do it. And falling behind in housework, leaving something undone, making a mistake—all of those things continued my feeling of failure, that I was unworthy.

> **Perfectionism is a problem when it starts to control your life and prevents you from enjoying it.**

I have always struggled with the normal daily activities of life. Trying to balance kids, their extracurriculars, my hospital shifts, overflowing linen closets, and the never-ending list of things that keep me up at night isn't easy. I have a hard time keeping up with it all. Actually, I suck at it.

After years of struggling and beating myself up over my inability to be the perfect woman, it turns out I'm not the perfect woman. I am a real one.

The Day My Perspective Shifted

I had fallen while wakeboarding hundreds of times. Wakeboarding is kind of like snowboarding, but you do it on the water, being pulled by a boat. I don't know what was different this time, but after I fell, I instantly knew something was seriously wrong.

It was my leg. I thought maybe my knee had popped out of place. I had seen elbows and shoulders popped back into place at work, so without even thinking, still underwater, I straightened my leg out as hard as I could, trying to pop my knee back into place. The white-hot pain was excruciating, and that attempt to fix it didn't do anything. My life jacket lifted me up out of the water, and I yelled, "I'm hurt!" My husband, who later said he thought I was joking, had to pull me back onto the boat. My leg wasn't working.

As I sat in the boat looking at my leg, it didn't make sense. The pain I felt was intense, but my leg looked fine. I was searching for an obvious deformity or swelling. There was nothing. But I felt like my knee was falling apart from the inside—and it turned out I was right.

I had broken all three bones in my leg, torn every ligament, and damaged my muscles and nerves. My world changed in an instant. I couldn't walk. I spent the next six months in bed, with physical therapy three days a week to learn how to walk again. I was in constant pain. I needed my husband's help with everything, even in the bathroom. He had to lift me and sit me on a shower chair. For my twenty-sixth birthday, I decorated my new walker with colorful tape.

All the things I had spent the last ten years stressing about were now *impossible* for me to do. I was lying in bed in pain, unable to get up and do the most basic of mom things. But instead of worrying about someone judging me, I cried because I couldn't tuck my two-year-old baby in at night or give him a bath. I couldn't play with him, and the thing I wanted most in the world was to be able to walk to the kitchen and make his favorite meal, his daily peanut butter sandwich. That same peanut butter sandwich that I was so irritated about making last week. I had been annoyed that he refused to eat anything else. He wouldn't even let me put jelly on it. But now, I didn't care what he ate. I didn't care if the house was a mess. I didn't care what the kitchen looked like. I just wanted to stand in it.

During that half a year in bed with pain that prevented me from moving my leg, all I could really do was think. I thought about how I took walking for granted. I thought about my family and the experiences I wanted to have with them. I thought about all the things I would do differently when I could walk again. I never once thought about how messy my closet was.

And I realized that if I found myself stuck in bed again, I wouldn't care about the messy house or what my coworkers thought about me. You hear the phrase *deathbed*, and it sounds like a terrible thing. But I started to imagine it as the end goal. I imagined a ninety-nine-year-old me, stuck in bed again, looking back on my life. If I used my ninety-nine-year-old self to guide me, my priorities changed. The unfinished housework and my cellulite didn't make me feel bad about myself. A clean house and toned legs weren't my ninety-nine-year-old self's idea of success.

I used to walk into the living room and see all my couch cushions torn off and thrown about. There would be old dishes on the coffee table and Legos and toys scattered everywhere. I could never find my car keys, my youngest only had one shoe, and we were always running twenty minutes late. I would get upset and think to myself, *When will I ever get my life together?*

It's been almost ten years since I was stressed with a toddler, and when I look back at those days, I don't think about how I was a mess who couldn't keep it together. I remember all the beautiful memories we made and how precious it was to rock my babies. I don't think about what I used to think about when I would tear myself apart. I think about the good things.

So, what would be important to my ninety-nine-year-old self? If I looked at my life through her eyes, I would not just

14

be looking at a chaotic mess. I would be looking at memories. She would tell me that I do have my life together. A life full of family and love. What I would be looking at is proof of a life well lived.

I am a perfectionist. I still get stressed out when the dishes and laundry are overflowing. I'm still a high achiever, and I like to be productive. But instead of letting those things define my worth or constantly trying to improve myself until I'm living my best life, I just want to enjoy this life I am living.

> **Instead of constantly trying to improve myself until I'm living my best life, I just want to enjoy this life I am living.**

This perspective shift was life-changing for me. I started viewing my home as a place to make memories instead of a place to make magazine-worthy. I started giving myself grace and praising myself for the hard work I had done instead of criticizing myself for what was still unfinished on my to-do list. I started looking at myself through the eyes of my children, not the eyes of strangers in the grocery store. I found the courage to show up imperfectly and let that be good enough.

My perspective shift was born through hardship, but it doesn't have to be that way. I'm guessing you can relate to many of these same feelings. I'm going to share my story and the breakthroughs that led to this perspective shift, and I hope they lead to your own perspective shift too. Let's unravel the expectations about motherhood and release them so we can be whoever we are today—and enjoy life.

REFRAME YOUR MINDSET

1

Perspective Changes Everything

Life is not the same for you and me. We perceive the world differently because we have different perspectives. What makes one person laugh can make another person cry. What discourages one will motivate another. Two people can live through the exact same experience and perceive it to be completely different. We don't have the same desires, hopes, or opinions. We can't all like, use, or enjoy the same things. How we perceive the world depends on what we see and what we hear. If we consider things from a different point of view, we can see things differently, we can hear new sounds, and our perspectives can change.

I like to think I'm tough in many ways, but I am miserable when it comes to the cold. I live in Oklahoma. We get all four seasons here, but our winters are mild if you compare them to winters up north. We never prepare for winter. When it does snow, the whole state shuts down. When it doesn't snow, schools sometimes close just because it's too cold to wait for the bus. Just stating the fact that schools are closed because it hit fifteen degrees can cause a major eye-roll re-action in people who live in places where that sounds like a warm winter day.

One person could consider fifteen degrees too cold to go to school, while the other person could consider it to be a nice break from the actual cold. These are two different percep-tions of the same temperature. Neither viewpoint changes the temperature. It's still fifteen degrees. But the life experi-ence changes the perception of it.

I feel most like myself in the summer. I like to be outside. All my favorite things in life happen in the sunshine. The cold weather feels physically painful to me. For years, I spent each winter season grumpy and unproductive. I would sink into the couch on my days off and just want to stay there. I couldn't do any of my favorite things because walking outside made me miserable. When it finally warmed up, I felt like a whole new person, and a giant wave of energy would rush over me.

One year, while feeling angry and unmotivated on the couch, I realized what I had been doing. I was spending each winter miserable, hoping for spring. That's an entire season of the year I was wishing away. When you add that all to-gether, it's an entire season of my life. I cannot fully enjoy life if I wish away a fourth of it.

I wasn't sure what to do, but I knew I needed to do some-thing. It was a big learning curve with trial and error to find ways to feel happier in the cold. Because of the environment I grew up in, I didn't realize the difference warm clothes would make. It sounds silly, but most people I know don't ever wear a winter coat. I didn't even own one. We would just do this mad dash to the car, moan about how cold it was, and then run inside to wherever we were going.

On my way to reaching my new goal of enjoying winter, my first step was wardrobe. I bought thermal pants, a big coat, warm hats, and gloves. I started wearing them when I went outside, and suddenly I wasn't so miserable. Shocking, I know. I realized I could go outside and stay out there if I had the right clothes on. It seems like such a simple concept, doesn't it?

I started spending fifteen minutes outside every day, no matter how cold it was. Even when I felt horrible and unmotivated, I got up, put on my coat and gloves, and went outside. I was amazed at the difference it made in my attitude. I don't know why it took me so many years to figure it out. Fresh air feeds my soul every spring, summer, and fall. Then I deprived myself of it for months in the winter and wondered why I felt bad.

After a few weeks of spending fifteen minutes a day outside, I found myself looking forward to that time. I was excited to put on my cozy socks and big coat. Going outside felt like an escape from the real world. But the more time I spent outside, the more I realized it wasn't an escape at all.

Outside is the real world. The trees, the creeks, the grass, the birds, all of those things are very real—much more real than what I stare at on a screen inside. Spending fifteen minutes outside each day reminded me to pull myself out of my bubble and look around. I get so caught up in my day-to-day life, I can forget that there is a whole world out there, just on the other side of my door.

When I stayed on my couch, my perception of winter was dark and depressing. When I physically moved, went outside, and looked around, my perception of winter completely changed. I found beauty in it. The weather didn't change; how I felt about it did.

I was so excited about my winter revelation that I started sharing it online. I would get on Instagram each day and share a clip of spending fifteen minutes outside. I would get responses from people I didn't know informing me that where I live isn't cold. It is colder where they live. I even had people laugh at me for wearing so many clothes. They called me ridiculous and dramatic. I was very much aware that colder places existed. But the fact that colder places existed didn't change the way I felt when I was cold.

One person's experience does not shape the experience of others.

One person's experience does not shape the experience of others. My experience doesn't shape yours. I have to keep reminding myself of this, because it is so easy to judge someone when I'm looking at their choices through the perspective of my own life. And it's even easier to compare myself to someone and feel inadequate if I don't move and broaden my horizons.

You Can Shift Your Perspective

I work as a travel agent from home, planning vacations for families. I have learned so much about people's perspectives at this job. What one person considers to be amazing, another person believes is awful. These differing viewpoints don't make one person right and the other wrong. They are both right about what they consider to be a waste of money. It's their perspective.

I walked into a "value" hotel room with a group of travel agents a few years ago. We were all staying there together. I loved the room. I'm a "value" kind of girl. To me, the room was the perfect size and the perfect price and had everything we needed. But to one of the girls who walked in behind me, it was the smallest hotel room she had ever been in. She said she felt claustrophobic just standing there. What I saw as charm and convenience, she saw as too small and unimpressive. The room was the same, but we described it completely differently. Our opinions didn't change anything about the room. Our perspectives were different because they were based on our personal experiences with hotel rooms. That didn't make one perspective better or worse than the other.

If we have had a bad experience with something, we can form a negative perception of it. When I am in a situation in which I feel bad, I have learned that shifting my perspective helps me feel good. I have always hated cooking. I would use all my energy searching for recipes, grocery shopping, and researching definitions of words like *sauté* and *broil*. When it was time to actually cook the meal, I was already exhausted.

Making dinner stressed me out. Things would burn, and I would make a huge mess. Nothing ever turned out quite like I expected it to. When it was time to eat the food, I didn't even like it. My kids especially didn't like it. My husband would eat it, but that didn't make me feel better at all. He would eat *anything*.

Repeatedly trying and failing at cooking made me want to give up. Knowing I was bad at something made that perfectionist voice inside of me tell me that I shouldn't try at all. Why would I want to put in so much effort for something that would make me feel like a failure and then cause me to have to clean up a big mess? I knew there were people who loved to cook. They found joy in it. People built entire careers around it. If they could enjoy it, why couldn't I?

I started my research. This wasn't easy to do. When you search for easy recipes online, you will find a lot of blog posts that wouldn't fall anywhere near what I would describe as easy. But with hours of work and weeding through words and ingredients I had never heard of, I finally found some recipes I could make on my own. Crock-Pot meals that allowed me to throw things together and basically forget about them began my perspective shift on cooking. Today, I still wouldn't call myself a good cook, but I have been able to take cooking off the list of things I hate most in this world.

We can shift our perspectives. We can broaden our horizons. We can be empathetic toward others who view the world differently. We can learn to be grateful for what we have instead of wishing for what someone else has. We can do all of this by seeking out new perspectives through questioning what makes us uncomfortable. The more you learn, the more your perspectives shift and grow.

Ashley Campbell is a woman I admire who writes a blog called *Under the Sycamore*. In a blog post from 2017, she describes some of the challenges she faced with her daughter who was born with a cleft lip and palate.[1] A cleft palate occurs when the tissue at the roof of the mouth does not form together, essentially leaving a hole that can make eating impossible and can lead to a long list of struggles and complications. Ashley's daughter underwent three surgeries and had years of therapies before ever eating solid food. For years she could only drink smoothies from a special bottle. On top of caring for and feeding her other children, Ashley would make all the smoothies and pack and prepare the bottles every day.

When they were out in public, she would get dirty looks from people who thought her child was too old to be using a bottle. Instead of pausing to consider why an older child may be drinking a smoothie from a bottle, people were quick to judge and used their own experiences to make conclusions. If they had heard her whole story, they could have learned about this medical condition and been able to shift their perspective, which could have helped them be more understanding and could have prevented them from sending a dirty look to a mother in the future.

We can learn by listening to stories from people who live and believe differently than we do. It's easy to judge people when they do things differently than us. If we disagree with someone, we tend to stick a negative label on them without trying to understand their reasoning. When we listen to different viewpoints with the goal of learning why instead of trying to change their opinions or actions to match ours, we learn so much about the world. When we learn how other people live and experience life, it helps us learn more about how we experience life, and it can completely shift our perspective.

You'll notice, too, that I never say to *change* it. Because you can't change what is uniquely your perspective. You *can* shift how you feel about it and how you feel about yourself by understanding other perspectives and broadening your horizons.

Get In Touch with Your Ninety-Nine-Year-Old Self

Our perspectives impact how we feel about the world and our role in it. My sister and I are ten years apart. I am older, so naturally, I am always giving her advice. Almost ten years ago, she was fifteen and I was twenty-five when she started telling me about some mean-girl drama that was playing out at school.

Fifteen-year-old girl drama sounds different when you are twenty-five. At that point, I didn't talk to a single person I went to high school with anymore. I'd had my share of drama back then, but none of it mattered at twenty-five. I couldn't remember what the fights were about or even some of the girls' names. A lot happened between fifteen and twenty-five.

As kindly as I could, I tried to explain this perspective to her. She was stressed about a lot of things—being a teenager is hard—but I encouraged her not to take it too seriously because what was happening now would be hard to even remember ten years from now. I told her to think back to when she was five. I asked her to remember the things she stressed about back then. Then I asked her how much those five-year-old worries and stresses mattered today. She said they didn't at all. I compared that to the way I remembered being fifteen. Fifteen was an entire world away.

The amount of change I experienced between five and fifteen was similar to the amount of change I experienced between fifteen and twenty-five. And that's when my sisterly advice slapped me in the face.

I asked myself, if all of this is true, does that mean my twenty-five-year-old stressors and worries won't mean this much when I am thirty-five? Will they feel a world away? Will I change again over the next ten years? Shouldn't I take this same advice I am giving my sister?

The answer to that was yes. My problems from my early twenties feel a world away a decade later. As I think back to my first ten years of marriage, or my time raising small kids, do I remember the stress I felt about the dishes in my sink? No, I don't. Even last month's mess doesn't bother me today. So I know today's mess won't bother me next year.

When I look at life with a zoomed-in view, I'm not seeing the big picture. I feel overwhelmed. Zoomed in, I focus on all the ways I think I am failing because I am not living up to my picture-perfect idea of who I am supposed to be. When I take a step back, out of my to-do list, out of my stress, and look at my life through the eyes of an older me, a wiser woman with a broader perspective on life, I realize I am giving too much of my attention to the small things. In our daily lives, we will be faced with struggles that we must navigate through, but with a zoomed-out perspective, it's easier to let go of the small stuff. Then I can give more of my attention to the things that will matter to me in ten years.

When I take a step back and look at my life with a big-picture kind of view, it's easy to see what is important and what isn't. My relationship with my family will always be what really matters to me. Instead of attempting to zero out my work emails after din-

My expectations change when I shift my perspective.

ner, I can make the decision to spend that time playing a board game with my children. Ten years from now, I won't regret if a client had to wait an extra day for an email, but I could regret spending my evenings working instead of hanging out with my sons. When I'm at the end of my life, I don't think I will care about what clothes I wore or how much money I made. I will want to know that I had the strongest relationships with my family and that I enjoyed my life while I could. When I use my older, wiser self to guide me, my priorities are different. A clean house, organized closets, and super-toned legs aren't my goals anymore. My expectations change when I shift my perspective.

This might look different for you. You might be more driven by work or travel. And if your expectations for yourself differ from mine, or from anyone else's, it doesn't mean they are better or worse. Some people love the cold, some don't. Some people love budget over luxury, some don't. They are different opinions, and they can exist in the same space, but one is not greater than the other.

So, did telling my sister to take a step back and look at her problem through her twenty-five-year-old eyes change the situation? No. But it did help change how she *felt* about it. In daily life, it's easy to forget about the big picture. During stressful times, I have to mentally take a step back and remind myself about my older, wiser expectations.

When I'm running late and walking through my messy house, unable to find my keys, my kids are fighting, and I want to break down and cry, I have two choices: I can do the easy thing, the thing I have always done—stress, cry, yell, and wonder, *When will I ever get my life together?* Or I can make a different choice. I can take a step back. Move. Shift my perspective. Look at the situation from a different point of view.

Looking at my life through the eyes of ninety-nine-year-old me, I can choose gratitude instead of stress when I see dirt tracked throughout my house. I might immediately feel annoyed that I just cleaned the floors and now they are covered in dirt. But if I stop and take a breath before I turn angry, I can remember the big picture. That dirt on the floor means my boys have been outside living their adventures. It means the life I wanted has come true. It means today, right now in this house, I'm living my dream. Clean floors are great, but they won't bring me peace when I am old and looking back on my life. The memories of my boys living here will.

When I pull myself out of the stressful emotions and look at the reality of the situation, the world looks different. Instead of seeing the problems I face, I can see all the good things. When I look at the situation through the eyes of a wiser me, I see a family I love and a home I'm lucky to have. These are the things that will matter to future me.

My perspective is my reality. But perspectives can be shifted. We can shift our perspective with life experience, by learning about others and by choosing to look at things from a different point of view. Shifting your perspective will change everything.

Imagine you are ninety-nine years old, looking back on your life today. What does ninety-nine-year-old you have to say about your current struggle? Can she offer a shifted perspective? The situation won't change, but how do you feel thinking about it through her eyes?

What is important to your ninety-nine-year-old self? Use that as a guidepost.

Write This Down

- Picture ninety-nine-year-old you. Maybe you're sitting in a recliner crocheting or on the front porch watching children and chickens run wild. Write down whatever that looks like.
- Think about who you were ten years ago. Think about where you were, what you had accomplished, and what stressed you out. Pretend that you are the ninety-nine-year-old version of you. Write down how the older, wiser you feels about what your life looked like ten years ago.
- Still pretending you are ninety-nine, look back on the age you are right now. Write down how the older, wiser you would feel about how you are spending your time, what you have accomplished, and what brings you stress today.

2

Trying to Be Perfect
Doesn't Help Anyone

Deep in my perfectionism, I spent years comparing myself to people who I thought were better looking, smarter, or more fun to be around. I was constantly measuring myself against women around me who seemed like better moms, wives, and friends. Comparison took over my life when I tried to change myself to be more like them. I fell so deep into this practice of comparison that I found myself doing it with nearly every woman I saw. I competed with women who didn't know they were competing with me.

Instead of admiring the things I liked about them, my first instinct was to feel inadequate and competitive. Why are comparison and self-doubt my natural instincts?

Comparison Comes Easy

Comparison starts in childhood. I used to compare everything about myself to the other girls in school. I stopped wearing bows in my hair in first grade because none of the other girls wore bows. I wanted my hair to look like theirs. I compared my handwriting to that of the girls who could write in pretty cursive and make big bubble letters on poster boards. My bubble letters always looked deflated. I compared my shoes, my athletic ability, my height, my freckles, my weight, and anything else I could find to the other girls, all before I was ten.

There is a lot of advice out there that tells us to stop comparing.

Comparison is the thief of joy.

This is true and thought-provoking. But it never stopped me from comparing myself to someone.

Be yourself. There is only one you.

I heard this one a lot growing up. It never worked. Half the time I didn't know who I was, and the reason I was comparing myself so much was because I didn't like me. I didn't want to be like me. I wanted to be like her.

Don't compare your beginning to someone else's finish line.

Don't compare your behind-the-scenes to her highlight reel.

Community over competition.

How many of these types of phrases have helped you stop comparing yourself to others? They all helped me for about five minutes. I completely agree with each phrase. I like the images on Instagram when they come across my feed. I am 100 percent backing the validity of those statements. But when I find myself in a situation where I am comparing myself to someone else, those statements don't stop me. I just compare, say goodbye to my joy as it's stolen away, and wonder why my beginning is lasting longer than anyone else's. I think, *Who am I anyway?* And then I try to come up with a plan for how I can be as good as or better than whoever I'm comparing myself to. No phrase or artistic quote graphic can stop me from doing it.

So, How Do We Stop Comparing Ourselves?

Like everything you will ever do in your life, *not comparing yourself to others takes practice.* Comparing comes easily and naturally. No one had to teach me how to do it, and I was an expert at it by the first grade. Just telling myself to stop doing something I had been doing constantly from as far back as I could remember wasn't a great action plan. Instead, I had to come up with a real plan to help me fight the feeling of inferiority.

This plan has eight steps, which may seem like a lot. But it takes me all eight steps. I wish I could just write a pretty sentence and you would never compare yourself to someone again. But comparison runs deep, and it will take more than a sentence to help you climb your way out of that hole.

Step 1: Break it down and shift your perspective.

When you compare yourself to someone, break down what you are really feeling. If you think, *I wish I was that skinny* or *I wish I was that good at dancing/singing/soccer*, it means you don't feel like you're good enough. You might think, *I wish I had that many friends*, because you feel lonely. *I wish I was more like her* means you wish you were less like you. My body, my hair, my skills, they just aren't good enough. I'm not good enough. She is better.

Once you've discovered what it is you are really saying about yourself, write it down.

I can quickly think of the top two ways I have compared myself to other women in my adult life: my legs and my home.

33

My legs. Most of us have body image issues. I don't need to explain what that's like to anyone. My biggest one has always been my legs. I have never liked the shape of them, the way they have always touched when other girls have gaps. The way my pants fit. The way the cellulite continues to grow and get deeper. When I look at a woman in shorts and she has toned legs without visible cellulite or stretch marks, I instantly feel bad about myself.

So I write it down.

Her legs are flawless, and I hate my cellulite. I want my legs to look like hers.

With the surface issue written down, let's find the root of the problem.

If I get what I want, what will happen? If my legs do look like hers and all my cellulite disappears, what will change in my life? *I will feel confident wearing shorts in public.*

So, the root of this comparison is that I do not feel confident showing my legs in public.

Find the root of your problem and write it down.

Now let's shift the perspective using gratitude and edit those sentences.

With my injury that left me unable to walk, I spent a lot of time thinking about my legs. I learned a lot about the anatomy of my leg. I cried a lot of tears over the what-ifs that my orthopedic surgeon was handing me. There were a lot of scary words tossed around. I spent all my time wanting the pain to go away. All I wanted in the whole world was to be able to get out of bed and walk to my children. I wanted to be able to get up and do anything. I never once thought about my cellulite.

When ninety-nine-year-old me looks back on my legs today, she isn't going to think about my cellulite. She is going to remember fondly how I chased kids around and walked all over the neighborhood with them every Halloween. She is going to remember that time I hiked a volcano. So, I am going to flip this comparison problem around using her perspective.

Her legs are flawless, and I hate my cellulite becomes *Her legs are flawless, and mine are working.*

My legs can take me wherever I need to go. I can get up and do things for my kids. Yes, her legs are flawless to the eye; mine are flawless to my soul.

This takes practice, so let's do it again.

Her house is so much prettier than mine. My house looks old and like it was thrown together cheaply.

To find the root of the problem, I ask myself, *What if I get what I want? What if I get the home of my dreams? What will change?* I will be happier for a moment looking at newer, prettier things. I won't be embarrassed to have people over or show images of my home online.

So, the root of my problem is wanting nicer things and the pride of showing them off. I don't love this about myself. Let's shift that perspective. Quick.

Before we ask ninety-nine-year-old me, let's look at the house of a younger me: nineteen-year-old me, living paycheck to paycheck, struggling in a tiny apartment with a two-year-old, wondering if life will ever get easier. She would think my current home is amazing. Just the fact that I have one is her dream come true. Plus, it has three bedrooms, two bathrooms, a closet full of clothes, and a yard for kids to play in.

I know ninety-nine-year-old me won't look back and think about the way my house didn't measure up to the influencers' houses I currently compare mine to. I know that with certainty, because when I look back at nineteen-year-old me, I don't wish my apartment had been bigger or nicer. I don't wish my design skills had been better. I am just amazed at how I kept moving and taking care of my son. I am proud of how I was there for him and provided for him. Ninety-nine-year-old me is going to feel that way about me now. I just know it.

So, I will rewrite those sentences using wisdom and gratitude.

Her house is so much prettier than mine. But my house is all I need. I have a safe place to raise my kids, and I am so grateful for that. One day I will look back on this house with so much nostalgia. I am going to enjoy it while I am here.

Step 2: Let her win.

Comparison can become like a competition. We compare ourselves to the person we have put on a pedestal and feel down about ourselves because she does it better. *She is better than me, and she is winning at this thing.* Well, let's be real here. Maybe she is. Maybe she has prettier hair and is the best dancer and has tons of friends. Maybe she is beating you in that thing you wish you were better at. Maybe she is winning at life. So, let her.

Let her win. *Let her be better.*

Let her be the absolute best. Let her be prettier than you. Let her be skinnier. Let her be stronger, cooler, nicer, neater, more popular, funnier, more creative. Let her be the best at whatever she is the best at. Even if it's all the things. Even if she is better than you in every single area of life, just let her.

You aren't living her life. You are living yours. And when you waste your time trying to live up to someone else's life, you are throwing away your own. God created you a certain way. He didn't create you to be just like her. He created you to be you. Yes, you can better yourself in all the ways you want to. But better yourself. Focus on you, not her.

I didn't think I had a problem with wanting to be the best until the idea of letting someone else win felt so incredibly freeing to me. The idea that I can just let other people be better feels like I'm taking pressure off my shoulders. When I decide being the best isn't on my goal list, conquering comparison gets a lot easier. I did a deep dive on my life to try to figure out where this desire to be better was rooting from.

> When you waste your time trying to live up to someone else's life, you are throwing away your own.

I want to be the best. I don't want to admit that, but it's the truth. I don't like seeing other people surpass me; I don't like failing. I like to win. I'm a competitive person. When I was a kid, I had a lot of success with basically everything I tried. I auditioned for a play and got the part. I performed in a speech arts competition, and I won first place. I ran for office in fifth grade and was voted president of my school. I sang in front of my church; everyone told me how wonderful I was. I had a lot of success, and it came easily. So later, when I didn't have success, failure hit hard. Real hard.

Even when I was the best, that high of winning only lasted for a minute. I was instantly back to comparing myself. Wondering if anyone was mad that I had won. Wondering if I was really the right person to be president of the school. Wondering if anyone was going to find out that I didn't actually know what I was doing. Winning and being the best didn't help my comparison problem.

Once I achieved the goal I had created through comparison—whatever it was I thought would make me worthy—it didn't suddenly make me feel whole or better about myself. I would replace that issue with two new things about myself to compare to others. This was a never-ending game that I would always lose. And that is hard for someone who likes to win.

When I became a nurse, the comparison problem intensified. Now people in my life were tearing each other apart for not being the smartest person in the room. Experienced nurses were judging the new ones on their intelligence and skills. But we were new. We didn't really have intelligence or skills yet. It was the place to fake it until you make it.

There was a nurse I looked up to. She just seemed to have it all together. She was great at her job. She was confident. She never got stressed out. She always knew what to do, and she was just so smart. She had only a few more years of experience than I had, so I kept thinking I would catch up to her knowledge and skill level, but as time passed, when I compared myself to her, I never felt like I was reaching her expertise. I've never felt more like an imposter in my life.

I thought, *I'm just not as smart as she is.* I found myself harboring all this resentment toward someone I actually admired. When I failed in front of her, I felt extra embarrassed. I imagined she thought I was really dumb. She was a nice person, but we weren't friends. We had very different lifestyles, and I always felt like she didn't like me. When I was around her, I felt self-conscious and like I was bad at my job.

One day, I was just fed up and over it. I knew deep down I had some weird, unhealthy feelings toward her and that they were all created in my head. She had never done or said anything to me to suggest she didn't like me. She hadn't called me an idiot, as far as I knew, and I was tired of feeling that way about someone I really looked up to.

We were alone, scheduled together in triage, and I sat down next to her and said, "I think you are amazing at your job. You are just so smart. You know so much about every patient that comes in here. You always know what to do.

I feel like an idiot half of the time. I feel like I don't know what I am doing, and I wish I could be more like you." I just word-vomited and put it all out there.

She responded with something I never thought I would hear her say: "I have felt that exact same way too. I feel pretty confident about a lot of the things we do here because it's the same stuff I have done every day for the past few years. But I still feel like I don't really know what I am doing sometimes." That blew my mind. She was the epitome of intelligence to me, and she was admitting she related to me on a level I never thought she could.

She told me her knowledge base was larger than mine because she had worked in other departments. She explained to me that it was her experiences in different areas that helped her be a better nurse. It was stuff I wouldn't have easily learned working as an ER nurse because it was stuff only floor nurses did, which had helped her in the situations where I felt completely lost and like an imposter.

It was like she gave me permission in that moment to be who *I* was as a nurse. I no longer felt like I needed to catch up to her. All of a sudden, I was happy with letting her be better than me. She had a lot of experience I didn't have because she had worked in a completely different world than the emergency room. ER was all I knew. I stopped trying to be the expert at everything and decided to focus on myself, growing my knowledge base with the patients I did see and my nursing practice as a whole. I stopped comparing myself to her, and I became a much better nurse for it.

Deciding to be okay with someone else being better than you is like taking off a two-hundred-pound backpack that you have been carrying around and letting weigh you down. Letting someone be better at getting dates or having nicer clothes or the cleanest house or the best-dressed kids doesn't mean she is a better person. It means she is really good at that thing. And that is okay.

Step 3: Focus on your path.

When you decide to let her be better, it doesn't make her more worthy. It gives you permission to just be where you are. If the girl you compare yourself to wants her story to be about simultaneously juggling motherhood, housekeeping, a full-time job, and being president of the PTA all while posting perfectly curated images on social media, let her. Let her be the main character she wants to be in her story. Don't try to copy her story; write your own.

Speaking of stories, consider the Disney princesses. Cinderella is courageous and kind. She has wishes and dreams and the whole thing. It makes for a great movie. She comes from nothing and ends up with the prince and a giant castle and lives happily ever after. But that doesn't take anything away from the other princesses. They have different stories. Cinderella's happy ending doesn't change anything about Snow White's.

Each of these fairy-tale characters has their own story. Their own highs and lows. While a lot of their stories have very similar themes and endings, their journeys and life experiences are very different. Can you imagine if they spent time comparing themselves to each other? If Cinderella felt bad about herself because she couldn't grow her hair as long as Rapunzel's?

When someone else is doing worse than you, does that make you better? When someone else is doing better than you, does that make you worse? We tend to look at it that way. Women seem to want to race toward the top. It's as if we believe there are only a few spaces for women in the world and we want to beat all the others to them. When we see another woman get something we want, we might immediately feel defeated. *She's killing it and I'm not.*

Being the best at something doesn't make someone a better, worthier person. That girl you are comparing yourself to is running down her own path. She might be racing. But it's her own path that she is taking. And she is focused. She is winning her race. You don't have to race with her. You probably weren't invited to her race. And if she does ask you to compete, you don't have to sign up for it. That is her race. Her path. She is going to win because it's hers.

You have your own path. If you want to race, don't focus on catching up to her; beat your own best time. Or don't race at all. Stroll. Take the scenic route. Your path might be windier, more uphill, with dangerous cliffs, and you're just trying not to fall off. Her path might be straight. It might even be downhill and easy. If that's the case, she's going to get there faster.

It may not be fair. Life usually isn't. Some paths are easier than others. Your path might have more to see. You might have more to do along the way. Stop trying to beat the run time of a girl who is on a completely different path than you. Let her win her race. Allow yourself to be different. Focus on your feet. Take a break and smell a flower. This path was built for you.

Step 4: Be the big sister.

Imagine your little sister, your daughter, or whoever it is that you truly want nothing but the best for. When my sister kicks butt at something, I am completely overjoyed. I am her number one fan. She is a competitive cheerleader, which is something I tried to be at one time in my life, and basically, I sucked. I couldn't jump. I wasn't flexible enough. But this girl kills it. She competed at Worlds in high school. She was recruited via Instagram by a college who gave her a huge cheerleading scholarship. She went on to win two national championships. And there has never been a single moment I felt competitive with her or hoped she would fail.

I've always wanted the best for my sister. I don't have to tell myself to feel that way or remind myself not to compare myself to her. My desire for her to succeed comes naturally. I love her. If my little sister succeeds, all I feel is pride. If she is succeeding, I am succeeding. So, why doesn't it come naturally for me to want the best for everyone else? Why is competitiveness my natural behavior toward women I don't really know?

I have some natural-born instinct that pushes me to jealousy before excitement for another woman who is beating me at something. So I decided to shift my perspective and pretend the girl I am comparing myself to is my little sister. When I feel jealousy start to creep in, I stop and take myself out of the emotion of it. I look at that girl as if I am her big sister. If she were my sister, I would be overflowing with pride and happiness, and I would be inspired to keep going for whatever I want.

Step 5: Turn envy into admiration.

When I remove the competition, when I decide that I'm okay with not being the best, first of all, I get happier. I can just be happy for the one who is killing it. But also, I can admire her. I can learn from her. There is a huge difference between admiration and jealousy. So, when you find yourself feeling jealous, ask yourself why. What is it about this person that makes you feel jealous? What are you comparing yourself to?

If someone else has something I want, the very fact that she has worked toward that thing is usually the evidence I need to know that I can work for it too. Take writing a book, for example. I have dreamed of having a book published for over five years. I faced several rejections while I watched other women I didn't know get book deals. That was hard. But instead of letting that envy eat away at me, I used it as a tool to keep going.

Admiration can be a great tool. You can use it as motivation to get you somewhere you want to be.

I decided to admire the work they had put in, and I let that inspire me to work just as hard. So, do that mental work. Stop those thoughts of comparison and replace them with either thoughts of gratitude or thoughts of inspiration. Admiration can be a great tool. You can use it as motivation to get you somewhere you want to be.

Step 6: Don't chase accomplishments; find contentment.

I spent the last several years trying to grow an Instagram following. At first, I wanted to grow my account because I saw something missing from the accounts I followed. I saw people who were interested in the things I was interested in— home decor, parenting, DIYs—but all the people putting out the content I wanted to watch portrayed picture-perfect lives. I couldn't relate to them. I was always looking for someone who struggled to keep everything together, someone I could relate to. I couldn't find that person. So I decided to be the person I was looking for.

I started to share about things like my top-three list (more on that in chapter 6), and I got amazing feedback. People were telling me that what I was writing was actually making a difference in their lives. That's when I knew I wanted to write a book. I started researching what it would take. I learned that if you have a social media following, it is so much easier to get a book deal in the nonfiction world.

I'm a researcher and I love a good project, so when I realized this new goal, I was all in. I spent hundreds of hours reading about how to grow a social media account. I paid for online classes. I spent so much time researching that I should have a social media degree. And what I learned worked. For about a minute.

It was a ton of work for me to grow my account. I would spend up to twenty hours a week just trying to gain followers. That's a part-time job in itself. I worked my butt off, and I watched accounts that started after mine skyrocket past me. The comparison game was strong.

While trying to grow this thing, I quickly learned that there was never going to be a number of followers that made me feel valid. In the beginning, I followed a girl who had seven thousand followers. I remember thinking, *Wow, that is so many! If I could just have seven thousand followers, that would be more than I would ever need.* Then I did it. I hit seven thousand followers, and to my surprise, it did not feel anything like I thought it would. I decided I needed ten thousand followers to feel like my account was legit. I hit 10K and it felt cool. For a day. A day later, I started feeling like I needed 20K.

And that's when I realized—*it will never be enough.* If I am chasing a number, I will never catch it. It has to be about something deeper than that.

You probably aren't trying to grow an Instagram account, but chances are, you've worked toward a goal and watched other people reach it easier and faster than you. And that is hard.

I have accomplishments. I graduated from college. I got my dream job as an ER nurse. I bought a house. And all those things brought me great joy when I accomplished them. But without contentment and a deeper purpose, that joy goes away. I was always looking for the next thing to accomplish.

But when I am chasing accomplishments or things or status, I will never catch them. I will never be done. There will always be more to chase.

If I can't learn how to find contentment today, I won't know how to find it later.

Accomplishments will not bring you inner peace or joy. If you can't be content with who you are today, exactly where you are, you won't be content once you reach that goal you are working toward.

Step 7: Control who you follow.

The world of social media is a crazy place. I think it's safe to say those of us who use it have a love-hate relationship with it. It's so easy to fall into comparison when you are looking at highly edited videos of someone's curated life. The truth is, with the newest iPhone and the right editing software, you could create an Instagram feed just as amazing as the one you are comparing your life to. No matter what kind of life you live.

There is so much I love about the internet. The community I have found. The inspiration I have gotten. The unending wealth of knowledge at my fingertips. But there are dark spirals I have found myself falling down too.

Social media isn't the only way to fall into a comparison trap, but it's the easiest. You can do it first thing in the morning before you even get out of bed.

Maybe it's the girl who always makes you feel bad about yourself. Maybe it's because she was mean to you in high school, and you feel angry every time you see her post something awesome. Maybe it's someone who is always making you feel jealous because of their extravagant lifestyle.

If you have people like that on your feeds, whose posts give you bad feelings when you see them, you should think about unfollowing those people.

You control who you follow. If someone you follow is causing you to compare, unfollow that person today. If it's someone you don't want to unfollow, try muting them so you don't see their posts.

Follow people you love and respect. People who make you smile when you see they are doing well. People who inspire you, who uplift you, who make you laugh. People you learn from. Unfollow everyone else.

Something I am embarrassed to admit is that I unfollowed the Bucket List Family for a time. I absolutely love watching their travels, but during a time when I couldn't leave the house and I had no money to go anywhere but to work, watching them live such an incredible life brought me down.

After you have worked through your comparison issue and worked on building your personal confidence, you might be able to go back to the ones you unfollowed and follow them again. I began following the Bucket List Family again after working through the root of my problem. And I am so glad because I really enjoy their content.

Maybe you'll realize you don't want to go back to following the people you unfollowed. That is okay. It doesn't have to be a personal thing toward them. You can do it for you. You are removing the triggers that make it too easy for you to compare.

Step 8: Remember that trying to be perfect doesn't help anyone.

When we compare ourselves to others, it's usually in an area of life where we feel like we are falling short. If we could be more like *that*, we would be closer to our idea of perfection. But think about the most perfect person you know or have seen online. Do you find yourself wanting to be friends with that person, or do you find that person to be a little annoying?

Those "perfect people" may be doing helpful things, but their "perfection" isn't helping you. Often, it makes you feel bad about yourself. But when people are vulnerable and have the courage to show their imperfections, you feel closer to them. It's like a breath of fresh air to see someone show up imperfectly. You want to be their friend. You relate to them, and it just makes you feel more normal.

Don't try to be like the girl no one can relate to. Trying to be perfect doesn't help anyone.

Stay Focused

When I couldn't walk, I had to drop out of those comparison competitions. One simple phrase made all the difference for me: Let her win. Letting her be pretty, letting her be smart, letting her be more fun to be around, letting other people be who they are and allowing myself to be who I am was freeing.

You don't have to be the best or do everything right. You can let other girls get there faster while you go at your own pace and enjoy the scenery.

So, what if instead of measuring yourself against others, you started appreciating what you like about them and letting it inspire you?

What if you stayed focused on your own path? You could end up going places you never would have gone if you were trying to follow someone else's.

Write This Down

Think about the part of you that you keep comparing to others. Let's break it down and shift your perspective.

- Write down what you wish was different about yourself and how it makes you feel.
- Write down what would happen if your insecurity became the thing that you are comparing it to.
- Using wisdom and gratitude, shift your perspective. Rewrite those sentences through the eyes of ninety-nine-year-old you.

Eight-Step Action Plan to Stop Comparison

1. Break it down and shift your perspective.
2. Let her win.
3. Focus on your path.
4. Be the big sister.
5. Turn envy into admiration.
6. Don't chase accomplishments; find contentment.
7. Control who you follow.
8. Remember that trying to be perfect doesn't help anyone.

3

Don't Let Opinions
Shape Your Life

Perfectionism can be rooted in the approval of others. Most of us grow up aiming to people-please. From the moment we are born, we are told to obey our parents. There is a deep-rooted desire in every child to gain their parents' approval. Next, we are taught to listen to our teachers. We are graded on our ability to meet others' expectations of us. As kids, we naturally crave positive reinforcement. Sometimes we carry that need for approval with us into adulthood.

When I am trying to perfect my life, I think that gaining the approval of others will help me get there. I believe that if they accept me, I will find self-acceptance. But people perceive us through their own life experiences, not through who we really are. And no matter who you are, there will always be people who don't like you. There will always be critics ready to criticize you.

If you are focused on pleasing the people around you, you are going to face disappointment and failure. Because you will never please everyone. I think people hear that phrase a lot and don't really stop to think about it. So let me say it again.

No matter what you do, you will NEVER please everyone.

People are going to place expectations on you and judge you when you don't meet those expectations. But we don't need to achieve greater things or change anything about ourselves to meet anyone's standard of perfection. Because we are not called to be perfect.

You Can't Avoid Criticism

Jesus was criticized. Mother Teresa was criticized. If they couldn't avoid criticism, neither can we.

Criticism is everywhere. People enjoy judging and criticizing others. It's a fun game for some. A critic may judge someone who believes or acts differently than they do. When someone judges another person for their different choices, it helps them validate their own life choices. Believing what someone else is doing is wrong helps them feel like they are right.

It could be something small, like the shade of lipstick you wear, to something big, like your beliefs. *I would never wear lipstick like that; it makes her look like she's trying too hard. I would never be so stupid as to believe in a God; I don't need a crutch in life just to deal with it.*

And while I wish the world was full of less-judgmental people, we don't live in a perfect world. We live in a world full of critics. No matter what you say or do, someone will always find a reason to criticize it, especially on social media. This became extremely clear to me when I decided that I wanted to start drinking more water.

I made the decision to drink a glass of water each morning while I waited on my coffee maker. It was a simple actionable step that was easy to take. I like to build new habits slowly. They are more likely to stick that way. And I knew that if I could master starting with one glass of water in the morning, it would eventually turn into my drinking a lot more water every day.

I opened my Instagram app and decided to tell the world about my new habit. I explained what I was doing and started filming myself with a glass of water every morning. That helped me keep myself accountable in those important, early habit-forming days. While, overall, the responses I got were encouraging me to keep going, I got other kinds of messages too. Messages like "You need to add electrolytes to that water" or "You are supposed to be drinking it at room temperature! That looks too cold!" "Add lemon! You need to always be adding lemon to the water!" "Add lime! Lime is better for you than lemons." "You shouldn't be drinking it that fast; you should sip it slowly." "You need to add flavor to your water or you won't stick with it!"

While I understand that they were coming from a place of wanting to be helpful, I felt criticized. I couldn't even drink a glass of water without being told that I was doing it wrong and needed to do better. Reading all the unsolicited advice didn't make me want to research better ways to drink more water; it made me want to quit and stop sharing altogether.

Sometimes we perceive what was intended to be a helpful comment as criticism. This is common. The person making the comment is trying to help you improve something you probably weren't looking to improve. You might internalize that as being judged when maybe they weren't judging you at all. I think we've all experienced this at one point or another with the women in our lives. Maybe they weren't actually judging you, or maybe they were. Either way, if you live in a world where you interact with other people, you can't avoid criticism.

That water-drinking situation was a great lesson for me. There are times when I feel criticized about things that mean a lot more to me than a glass of water. It could be something I worked hard on or believed in. When people tell me they don't like it or that I am doing it wrong, it easily hurts my feelings. Their opinions can leave me questioning myself and my choices. But when I think about the fact that I can't even drink water without being told I am doing it wrong, it helps me shift my perspective.

There is nothing I can do that will please everyone. No matter what I do, someone will tell me it isn't good enough. So instead of looking for outside approval, I need to look within. So I did. I didn't quit sharing. I kept drinking the glass of plain water. I knew it would be beneficial for me. After a couple of months, it became a habit. I was craving the water first thing in the morning. And like I thought it would, it eventually led me to crave more water throughout the day. I drink more water now than I ever did before. And I did it without the approval of anyone else.

The Weight of Criticism

You know in the movies, when the teenage girl is walking down the hallway of her high school and everyone is looking down at their phone, whispering to each other? It's obvious that they are all talking about her as she walks by. The girl puts her head down and keeps walking in shame or runs out of the school because she knows what they are saying. They are judging her.

I felt like that girl when I was in school. People talked about me. They judged me behind my back and to my face.

I was a pregnant teenager in a town with a population of about five thousand people. It felt like all eyes were on me. Strangers would walk up to me and tell me exactly what they thought. As if my pregnant stomach was somehow an invitation for them to let me know they disapproved of my choices.

The disgusted tone of voice every time I heard, "How old are you?"

The loud whispers, saying, "Oh my gosh, look how big she is."

The teacher who used to respect me but told my mom that I would never step up to raise a baby.

These things really hurt, especially the words from that teacher. I had really respected her opinion of me.

I was sixteen, trying to prepare myself to become a mother. What I never could have prepared myself for were all the judgmental opinions of the world. And they just got worse after my son was born. Everywhere I went, people I had never met would say, "That's just your little brother, right?" Or even ruder: "You shouldn't be raising that baby because you are a baby." I had a woman walk up to me in the mall to tell me she thought I should give my baby up for adoption so he could stand a chance.

I couldn't get on an elevator without judgment. I couldn't take my baby to the store without people demanding I explain myself to them. Any time I was in public with my child, people were rude to me. I am not exaggerating here. It was *every time*. But I was afraid to run to the store without my child too. I feared that if someone I knew saw me without him, they would think I was a stereotype, leaving my baby with someone else to raise him. I was overthinking every decision I made, weighing every choice against the potential criticism I would receive.

I felt a desperate need to prove everyone wrong. My life revolved around it. I felt like everyone was waiting for me to fail. And I couldn't fail. I loved my son more than anything. Looking back now, I can tell you with certainty that I was a good mom. If you met this kid now, you would agree. He is the most incredible teenager any mom could ask for. But when he was a baby, I was afraid the opinions of others would somehow lead to them taking him away from me.

I put so much pressure on myself because of that fear— way more than I ever did with my second child, who everyone was happy about because I was older and married. I had come up with the idea of what a successful mother would look like, and I wrecked myself trying to make it happen. I was trying to impress people I didn't even know. I was so concerned with the opinions of people who would never be a significant part of my life.

You need to drop the weight of all the criticism before it crushes you.

I share this story to let you know that I understand what it feels like to be criticized and to build a life around trying to change other people's opinions.

No matter what you do, you will face criticism. If you try to avoid it by shaping your life around gaining other people's approval, you are just going to be carrying those opinions and criticisms around with you. That gets really heavy really fast. You need to drop the weight of all the criticism before it crushes you.

Your Inner Circle

One of my favorite quotes by Annie Dillard is "How we spend our days is, of course, how we spend our lives."[1]

56

Write that down.

The way you spend your days is the way you spend your life.

If you spend your days worrying about what other people think of you, you will spend your life worrying about what other people think of you. Instead, you could just live your life. It's not your job to make someone else like you. If they want to think badly about you, let them.

If you believe in yourself, the choices you've made, and the path you've chosen, don't stop to second-guess what that girl from work might think. The only opinions that matter are the ones of those you are doing life with, and who is in this group looks different for everyone. It could be your spouse, your parents, or your best friend. But whoever it is, it's a small number of people, a select few that you trust completely. It's your inner circle, the people you would call if you broke down on the highway. If you wouldn't write them down as your emergency contact on a medical form, their opinion doesn't matter.

People who aren't living inside your circle don't know your story. They might know someone else's story about you. They might have written their own story about who they believe you are. But unless you have invited them into your daily life, they don't really know you. They aren't living with you day in and day out. They aren't who you call first to celebrate the big moments, and they aren't there to help you pick up the pieces when you're having a horrible day. They don't help you by running to pick up your kid when you won't make it in time. They aren't grabbing diapers from the store for the baby because you are too tired to get out. They aren't in your inner circle, so their opinion of you isn't based on truth. It's based on their perception of what they can see, and it's incomplete because they don't have all the details.

When someone outside of your circle shares a negative opinion about you, just throw it away. Do not let it take up space in your mind. That can be easier to do when you don't care deeply about the person criticizing you. But what if it is coming from someone close to you?

Let's be honest, sometimes we need to hear hard truths. If someone inside your inner circle tells you something that feels hard to hear, a conversation should be had. We can and should consider constructive criticism from the people who love us unconditionally.

But it isn't always constructive, is it? On Instagram, I asked people to tell me whose critical opinion they struggled with the most. Overwhelmingly, the answer was their mom and/or mother-in-law. I asked for specific examples of the kind of critical opinions they were struggling with. Most of them said, "my parenting style," "my decision to work full-time," "my decision to be a stay-at-home mom," or "she thinks my house is too messy."

So, what if it's your mom or your mother-in-law who has the critical comments? I'm so sorry if it is. You might have to realize that person isn't actually in your inner circle. The people in your inner circle should be the ones who support and encourage you. The ones you feel safest with. The ones who love you unconditionally.

The next time you stop to consider someone's negative opinion about you, first check to see if they are inside the circle.

Assuming Negative Opinions

I used to clean houses after class. Being seventeen with a baby, I wasn't a typical student at Tulsa Community College. Almost all of my peers were my mom's age, working toward a second career. I didn't exactly fit in. In my anatomy lab, there was a woman in my group who I admired, and I hung on every word she said. She basically embodied the kind of person I wanted to grow into. I didn't know anything about her, but she was smart and funny and a joy to be around.

In conversation, the fact that I cleaned houses came up, and this woman I admired laughed. She looked right at me and laughed out loud. She kind of coughed it away and changed the subject. That stung. I immediately felt shame about something I had previously felt proud of. With her one little laugh, she squashed me. That pain stuck with me for years.

We parted ways after that, and I tried to forget the whole event. I wrote her off as a rude person and moved on. Years later, I ran into her at work. She was a PICU nurse, and I was delivering a patient to her. When I saw her, I wanted to run the other way. I pretended I didn't recognize her, gave report on the patient, and turned to run as far as I could. But before I could go, she stopped me with a huge smile on her face.

She reintroduced herself to me, explaining that she remembered me from that anatomy class all those years ago. My heart was beating out of my chest. I did not want to be friendly toward this person who had hurt me deeply. While I was trying to decide if I should tell her I remembered her or pretend I didn't, she started telling me her story.

She had started community college at the age of forty, wanting a complete change in direction. She told me that she had also been a teen mom but took a very different path than I had. When she walked into that anatomy class and was put in a group with me, the sight of me made her feel deep feelings. I reminded her of herself when she was young. She told me she was so proud to see what I had accomplished as a teen mom and that I hadn't let that stop me. She called me a source of encouragement that kept her going.

That was not at all how I perceived her opinion of me. I stood there completely shocked. I thanked her for her kind words and told her how much they meant to me. Then I let her know that I remembered her, and I got up the courage to tell her about how I felt like she didn't like me because she'd laughed when I mentioned my housecleaning job. She instantly apologized. She let me know that her laugh was in no way judgment. She said she didn't remember laughing, but it would have been a "way to go, this makes me happy" kind of laugh because she was impressed that I was hardworking. She told me that the more she learned about me throughout that semester, the more she respected me. I had that very wrong.

I got really good at creating negative storylines in my head. I spent years getting negative opinions thrown in my face. It became like second nature to imagine those criticisms in every look, gesture, or laugh before they ever actually came. I started believing that everyone around me was judging me all the time. I started building up walls to protect myself from that pain. But those walls kept people out that I could have been friends with. I had mentally trained myself to believe that all new people didn't like me.

We spend more time worrying about people's negative opinions than they spend having those opinions.

I spent years working through always feeling judged. Years of counseling, reading books, and listening to podcasts and preachers talk about how I should handle other people's opinions. Over and over, I kept hearing the same advice: *People don't think about you as much as you think they do.*

60

That made so much sense to me. There have been actual studies done about this. People are mostly obsessed with themselves. Maybe they think something about us in passing, but they don't dwell on it. We spend more time worrying about their negative opinions than they spend having those opinions. We're giving more thought to it than they are.

This felt freeing. People don't think about me nearly as much as I think about their opinions. Believing this, I was able to let go of the negative emotions I had built up and the years of struggle with hating the way people perceived me. I was finally able to just let it go with the realization that most of it was probably in my head anyway.

So What If They Are Thinking About You?

After high school, I left that town thinking everyone hated me. The public image of me among my peers was bad. They didn't question any of the rumors they were being told or call me to ask for my side of the story. They made me feel very much like an outsider who was unwelcome in her hometown.

Years later, I had worked through those feelings. I thought I was probably overreacting because I was young. Yes, I did get hateful messages from some people, and others said horrible things to my face, but I was a teenager. There was no way everyone in school really hated me the way I thought they had. Most people probably weren't even thinking about me. I had made incredible strides with the way I felt about that. There was a time when I was actually afraid to stop at the gas station in town, but now I can go back to visit my mom without fear of harsh judgment. I mean, who do I even think I am? Most people from high school probably don't even remember my name, right?

Around a decade after I left school, I had the opportunity to go on a women's retreat. It was a two-night event in another city. I didn't have any friends going with me, so I was assigned a hotel room with a stranger. That was where I ran into Megan. Megan and I had gone to high school together. She was a year above me, and we never talked in school. But she had been friends with my high school boyfriend. And she remembered me.

She was assigned as my roommate. She was super friendly, and I really enjoyed spending time with her. She is someone I absolutely would have loved to have as a friend. One night, when we were up way too late talking about everything, my reputation in high school was brought up. She kindly asked me for my side of the story. I told her things had gotten really bad in my relationship. All my self-esteem was crushed, and I had felt stuck. It took me four years and some really drastic measures to finally gain the courage to leave. That wasn't the story she had heard.

She was being so nice, and I felt like I could be honest and open up, so I told her that when I found out she was going to be my roommate, I was nervous. I apparently hadn't worked through my issues as well as I thought I had. I still had a deep feeling that everyone from that town hated me. But I had done a lot of therapeutic work. I knew people didn't think about me nearly as much as I thought they did. I knew most of my feelings were probably just negative assumptions in my head.

But she didn't respond in the way I expected. She didn't confirm any of the therapeutic work I had done. Instead, she told me that she had hated me in high school, that everyone she knew had. They had all called me names, like "slut," and thought I was ruining my high school boyfriend's life. She said that when I got pregnant, I instantly became a slut in her mind but that she had never thought to consider my side of the story.

She had confirmed all the fears I had worked so hard to get past. But she said she realized she had no right to think the things she did about me. Specifically, the word *slut*. She said she knew other girls who were sexually active, but when I got pregnant, it was different in her mind for some reason that she couldn't explain. And she apologized for choosing to believe the worst about me without knowing me at all.

Opinions Are Not Facts

Megan's perception of me had been based on things she had heard, along with her own personal beliefs about what it meant for a girl to get pregnant in high school. But she didn't know me. We had never even spoken. She had thought she knew who I was, but her version of my story wasn't true.

Megan calling me a slut did not make me a slut.

Megan thinking I had made all the wrong decisions while trying to escape my relationship didn't make it true.

But Megan's opinions completely changed when she heard more of the story.

In my life, I have been called a lot of contradictory things. I have been labeled as the shy girl who needs to speak up and as the loud, annoying girl who needs to sit down. I have been called the nice girl and the mean girl. I have been told that I was respectful and obedient. I have also been told that I was rude and rebellious.

According to the opinions of others, my identity was always changing. But I wasn't actually changing. The opinions of me were.

Thoughts and opinions change; they cannot define you. Someone else's perception of you does not make you who you are. Don't let someone's opinions about you shape your life.

Imagine a celebrity or historical figure you admire. Maybe it's Harriet Tubman, Marie Curie, or Anne Frank. Maybe it's Dolly Parton or Taylor Swift. Whoever it is, think about that person. Think about the reasons you admire them. Now think about the people who don't like them. They tear them apart in the news, social media, or in history. If you can't think of anybody who doesn't like them, just do a quick online search. You'll find websites dedicated to the hatred. Someone out there has disliked the person you admire. Does their negative opinion change the way you feel about that person? Hopefully not. Because you have real reasons why you admire them.

It doesn't matter how awesome and fantastic and wonderful you are, there will be people who disagree with you and your choices. There will always be people who don't like you. That doesn't stop you from being awesome, fantastic, and wonderful. Their opinion of you does not define who you are.

If someone's negative opinion wouldn't change the way you feel about your favorite celebrity, don't let someone's negative opinion change the way you feel about yourself.

Why Do We Care What People Think?

We often care so much about what other people think because we care about other people. We value their opinions. We value them as people. It isn't a bad thing to care. It makes you empathic, and empathy is an admirable quality. But we have to learn how to value someone as a person while understanding that their opinion doesn't define us.

There are times in my life when it is incredibly easy not to give a single you-know-what about what someone thinks about me. For example, there have been countless times that, while working as a nurse, I have been hated by someone the moment I walked into their hospital room. I don't even have to open my mouth before I am being cussed at and threatened. I have had grown men get in my face and threaten to hurt me because I was doing my job.

There was once a mother who asked me for a warm blanket for her child. As I left the room to get the warm blanket, another child came in through the ambulance bay. This was a toddler who had just been found at the bottom of a pool. The paramedics were doing CPR as the child was rushed into a trauma room.

When a child needs CPR in the emergency room, it is a team effort. We are trained for it. We all have our jobs. I ran into the room and took my position. We take turns doing chest compressions, we start IVs, and we give medications meant to restart the heart. There is a lot going on, and all I am thinking about at that moment is trying to stabilize the child. We got his pulse back, but that was just the beginning of a very long road to his recovery. There are a lot of emotions with both parents standing there. You can imagine what that's like.

We spent about forty-five minutes working on him before I felt like my job was done and I could leave. I walked out of the trauma room toward the nurses' station. I probably needed a drink of water or just to stretch for a second after those events. Before I could get there, I was stopped in the hallway by a very angry mother. She started yelling at me. She called me incompetent and wanted to know where she could find the warm blankets since I obviously couldn't be trusted to do my job.

I hadn't brought her child a warm blanket. This mom thought I was an idiot. But her opinion of me did not make me feel bad about myself for even one second. Yes, it was incredibly frustrating, and I wanted to tell her where I had been and what I had been doing. There were times that I didn't respond to situations like this in the most mature way, and this time I pointed to the blanket warmer and sat down. It wasn't worth it to me. She didn't know the whole story. She fired me as her nurse because of my unapologetic attitude and requested someone else.

I didn't take any of her opinions to heart. Had she known the whole story, she might have felt differently. She wouldn't have been demanding a warm blanket; she'd be grateful her kid was breathing on his own. She would probably thank me for the hard and challenging work I was doing. But she didn't know. She judged me based on her perspective of waiting in a room for forty-five minutes for a blanket. From her perspective, I had abandoned her child in a cold room without caring about his comfort. But I didn't go home that day thinking badly about myself over her opinion. I knew her opinion wasn't based on fact.

It was kind of like when my son was three and told me I was the meanest mom in the world because I wouldn't let him ride his bike unattended down the street with the teenagers of the neighborhood. He thought he should have been allowed to roam freely with the big kids. But first of all, he was still riding a tricycle and never remembered to stop for traffic. Second of all, no. But his opinion that I was the meanest mom in the world didn't affect me because I knew what I was doing; I was keeping him safe.

When you are confident in your choices, it is easier to brush off critical comments. When someone is presenting you with negativity, center yourself back on the reason you made the choices you did. Live your life in a way that makes you proud despite what someone else will think about it.

We so often want everyone to just understand us. We believe that if they understood why we were doing what we were doing, their opinion of us would change. In some cases, that can be true. But it's not your job to make the world understand you. If it's someone in your inner circle, please do the work to explain yourself. But if it's anyone else, let them misunderstand you.

I decided to stop trying to control what everyone's perception of me was and let them believe what they wanted to believe. By doing that, I found a self-confidence inside me that had been dying to get out.

The World Is Wide

The world is full of different people. That's what makes it so beautiful. The world is wide enough for my inner circle and my outer circle. It's wide enough for the people who dislike me. I can be loved by some and hated by others. The hatred doesn't diminish the love. I can be the villain in someone's story and the hero in another person's. To live in a world where everyone loves you would be to live in a very, very small version of the world. And I don't want to do that. I want to explore it all.

There are so many people I strongly disagree with. And there are people who strongly disagree with me. They may hate this book. They may call me a sorry excuse for a writer. And that's okay. Someone will like this book. Both of those opinions can exist at the same time. People can hate you, and you can keep on living your best life. Because the world is wide enough to hold us all.

If I find myself worrying about other people's opinions, I remind myself to worry about my own, and I look at my life through the eyes of ninety-nine-year-old me. She isn't worried about what people are saying. She is concerned with the memories I am making and the core people I am surrounding myself with. When I am focused on that, I can easily let go of someone else's opinion of me. I am actively building my life, not theirs. This is the only life I get. I want to decide how to live it.

You can't control what people think.

Let people be wrong about you.

Let them misunderstand you.

Life is a lot easier that way.

Write This Down

- Draw a circle. Write the names of the people who are closest to you inside the circle.
- Write your biggest critic's name outside of the circle.
- Write down criticism that someone gave you that has been taking up space in your heart. Underneath that sentence, write down what ninety-nine-year-old you has to say about it. Listen to older, wiser you. Not the critic.

Mindset Tools
for Facing Criticism

You know that you are going to face criticism. Even if you cut every seemingly toxic person out of your life, you aren't going to get rid of negative opinions. Those are always going to find you. So prepare yourself. The tools you need to handle negative opinions are all part of your mindset. You may need to shift your perspective. You will need to put in a lot of work and practice. But if you do, you will be able to free yourself from the opinions of others and live your life the way you want to.

Don't Add to the Problem

You put out what you take in, so don't purposefully take in negative opinions. Don't seek them out yourself. You'll find enough without looking for them. If you have "friends" who are always mean to you, stop calling those people friends.

We think about what we fill our minds with. Whether you want to believe it or not, when we spend our time watching true crime TV, watching girls get snatched by serial killers, we are more likely to be afraid as we walk to our cars. When we spend our time consuming the Bible, we think about biblical things. When we stand in front of the mirror and point out our flaws, we are more likely to tear ourselves apart for the rest of the day. When we stand in front of the mirror and cite positive affirmations, we are more likely to think positive things throughout the day.

I'm highly affected by what I consume. Positive, uplifting music uplifts me. Angsty, depressing music makes me feel all the angsty, depressed feelings.

Don't purposely do things that you know will lead to negative thoughts.

Decide Who You Are

You must decide who you are before you let other people decide for you. The big question of *Who am I?* can seem very daunting if you are unsure. But even if you are unsure about who you are or what your purpose is, you know you better than anyone else does. You need to know who you are and who you aren't before people start throwing labels on you.

If you're like me, they will call you all of it over your lifetime. Some will say you're nice, some will say you're mean. Some will say you're shy, some will say you're loud. But those are opinions, not facts. Don't put weight on something as unstable as an opinion.

Write down a few things that you admire about yourself.

Maybe you have a heart for children or animals.

Maybe you always show up for work on time. You are dependable.

Maybe you are forgiving or brave or great at budgeting.

We don't need to achieve anything greater or change things about ourselves to meet anyone's standard of perfection. Because we are not called to be perfect.

Write down who you are.

Don't Explain Yourself

You don't owe anyone outside of your inner circle any explanations. Your full story is personal. It can be vulnerable, and everyone in the world doesn't have the right to know the intimate details about what makes you the way you are. You can save the whole story for those who are doing day-to-day life with you.

For much of my life, I felt the need to explain myself to anyone who had a negative opinion of me. Whether they thought I was a slut, incompetent, or someone who didn't know how to drink water correctly, I wanted to reach out to them and explain myself so they could understand the whole story. And I did that several times. But trying to change the mind of everyone who had a misguided thought about me became exhausting. I spent time thinking about it, crafting responses, and sharing those responses. Sometimes I'd get an apology, which felt satisfying in the moment. But sometimes I'd get an eye roll or a very troll-ish response. Either way, after the conversation, I didn't feel better.

I felt exhausted trying to explain myself to everyone all the time. So I stopped. Because I don't owe them an explanation. They are not part of my day-to-day life. If they want to be wrong about me, I'm going to let them.

Remember that you don't owe anyone explanations. If they want to be wrong about you, let them.

How to Respond When You Are Handed Criticism

It amazes me what people think is okay to say. With the increased use of social media, I have seen an overall decrease in manners. Have a plan for the next time someone tries to hand you a critical comment.

Take a Deep Breath

Don't dive in right away to defend yourself. Remember first of all that it's okay if someone is wrong about you or doesn't like you. Opinions do not define you.

Consider the Source

Is the criticism coming from someone inside your inner circle? If not, don't take it to heart. If so, is it meant to help? Or is it completely unhelpful? Is the comment meant to tear you down? Someone may say something that fills you with rage but was said with kind intent. If the person is in your circle, talk with them about the intent of their comment and how it made you feel. Consider the source and the intent behind the comment before reacting.

Remember Your End Goal

You can't please a critic. If you try to play the people-pleasing game, you'll always lose in one way or another. Whatever the comment is, people-pleasing isn't the end goal.

If someone is criticizing your parenting, what's your end goal? Is it to be accepted by that person? Is it to get the most likes and positive comments from all the moms in the Facebook group? Or is it to raise well-adjusted children?

You can't follow your beliefs, raise well-adjusted children, and please all the critical mothers out there. You can't have it all. Pause to remember your end goal before responding to the criticism.

Choose Your Response

I have three responses to criticism that I like to choose from: ignore, agree and add additional context, or be vulnerable.

1. Ignore

You can always choose to ignore critical comments. You don't have to entertain that person's negativity. You don't have to attend every argument you are invited to, and you don't owe anyone an explanation. I responded this way to the patient's mom who told me I was incompetent at my job. I was exhausted from doing CPR on a kid without a pulse. I didn't have the time or energy to care about her opinion.

You can walk away or respond with a simple statement, like "thank you." If the critical person wants to play a back-and-forth game with you, you can refuse to play. You don't have time for that. You need to spend your energy on productive things, and responding to that person's comment isn't worth your time.

2. Agree and Add Additional Context

When someone brings a rude comment to me, I have learned how to flip it around to make them sit in their own rude comment. I can do this by agreeing with them but adding additional context.

I am overly sensitive toward people telling me I look too young to do something. It's a me problem. It stems from my experience of being told I was too young to be a mom. What most people take as a compliment, I easily take as a rude comment that could ruin my day.

Sometimes, when I consider the source and the intent, I realize the comment isn't malicious, and I just say thank you and move on. But sometimes it actually is rude. It doesn't happen nearly as often as it used to, but I still look pretty young for my age, and some people act weird when they find out my teenager is my child. So I had to figure out a way to respond that would allow me to continue on with my day without getting pulled back into those old feelings of not being good enough for my kids.

A stranger once asked me how old my kids were, and I responded with sixteen and ten. Her face was covered in judgmental confusion. I am sure she expected me to say something like two and four. Instead of saying the normal thing about how I look too young to have a teenager, she started coming up with reasons why she wouldn't need to judge me. "Oh, are they your stepchildren?"

"No," I replied. "They are mine."

That's when she said it. "Wow, you look way too young to have kids those ages."

It wasn't the words she said—someone else could have said it in a different tone, and I would have just said thank you and moved on. But she said it in a tone of judgment and some desire to figure out my story so she could decide if she should be critical or just ask about my skin-care routine. I could tell she was being critical, and that tone made me want to respond. So I agreed but added additional context.

"I am too young," I said. "I got pregnant when I was sixteen."

"I am too young" became my go-to response when people commented on my appearance.

Her face was instantly covered with regret. She started apologizing to me. I didn't act upset. I told her she didn't need to be sorry. All I did was agree with her statement, and it left her feeling convicted about the judgment she had shown me. I was able to leave that conversation feeling satisfied with my response.

3. Be Vulnerable

Other times, and only times when I feel especially safe to do so, I get really vulnerable when I am criticized, and I respond to the criticism by being completely honest with how it made me feel. This forces the critical person to be immediately presented with consequences of their words. If someone is just being a bully, this is not a good tactic. But if it's someone who genuinely thinks they are helping you with their criticism, it can work really well.

If someone close to you says something to you about how you are doing something wrong in your house or with your children, consider getting vulnerable. I once had a female relative tell me that I was breastfeeding my baby too much. She said I was going to end up in the hospital with pneumonia from too much breastfeeding and that my baby would then starve because I wouldn't be able to breastfeed and he wouldn't be used to a bottle, so no one would be able to feed him.

Never mind the centuries of mothers feeding babies without bottles. Never mind the fact that my baby did use a bottle every time I went to work. The criticism doesn't always make logical sense.

But you can respond in a nonargumentative and vulnerable way, like "I feel like you don't think I am capable of making good mothering decisions. I feel like you don't trust me to take care of my own kids. That really hurts my feelings and makes me want to distance myself from you. Negative thinking and critical comments like that are not helping me at all. They're just making me feel really judged by you. I am doing the best I can, but I feel like I will never be good enough for you."

Instantly, they have to deal with the consequences of their comment. If you respond like that, it makes it awkward for the critical commenter. If you keep getting vulnerable, that person will start thinking twice before sharing criticism with you because they won't want to deal with the awkward aftermath.

Play the "Bullying" Game

Sometimes people criticize you because they want to bring you down. They don't care about you at all. They are bullies. Or internet trolls. They are looking for a reaction out of you. The mature thing to do is probably to ignore, but sometimes we want to respond. If you want to respond to a bully, do so by playing what I call the bullying game.

I taught this game to both of my kids, and they have some great stories about how they used it at school. Some *great* stories. This game may be intended for elementary school bullies, but it works on adults too. The goal of the bullying game is to make sure you do not get upset or give the bully the response they are seeking. If you get upset, they win. If you don't get upset, you win.

The point of the game is, each time the bully criticizes you, to respond with a descriptive compliment. It can be really funny.

The bully criticizes you. They say something like "That dress looks terrible on you," so you respond with "Your sweater is amazing and matches your beautiful eyes."

You just made it awkward for that bully. That was not the response they were expecting.

The bully then says something like "Your makeup is disgusting," so you respond with "Your smile shines like a million glittering diamonds."

Basically, you don't respond to the criticism. You don't let it upset you. The bully doesn't win. Instead, you respond in the exact opposite way of what the bully expects. The bully feels awkward. The bully gives up. You win.

It's a game. Is it the healthiest thing? I don't know. But it works. It especially worked for my kids in school. And you may have a few extended family members you might want to play it with over the holiday season.

Change Your Mindset

On the TV show *Gilmore Girls*, Emily constantly criticizes her daughter, Lorelai, to her face, so Lorelai comes up with a defense mechanism for this criticism. She shifts her mindset. She can't control her mother, but she can control her brain. So instead of feeling hurt and upset when her mother shares her disapproval, she starts finding the humor in it. She even buys home décor that she knows her mother will hate just to get the pleasure of the disapproving comment. When she is faced with the critical comment, she can respond by laughing. There may be someone in your life you are never going to please. Try finding the humor in it.

Get a Second Opinion

If something someone said is really sticking with you, ask your inner circle about it. Ask your husband or your sister or your mom. Ask your best friend. Your core people are the ones who matter. If it's a real problem, they will talk through it with you. If they think it's something you should let go, they are probably right. Let it go.

SECTION 2

EMBRACE WHO YOU ARE

4

Different Kids
Need Different Moms

Momming didn't come easy for me. No matter how hard I tried, I never felt like I was doing enough. Having a baby was hard. I was exhausted. Having a toddler and then a strong-willed preschooler was even harder. We were always late to everything, he wouldn't eat dinner, he had night terrors, and he never slept. So I never slept. There were so many challenges. As soon as I figured out a solution to one problem, there were three new problems. I couldn't keep up. I was failing miserably. I was forgetting everything, and the feeling that I wasn't doing enough consumed my waking thoughts.

I spent the first several years of my son's life researching how to be a good mom. I was so afraid of failing at it. I studied every parenting book I could get my hands on. I would highlight the entire book, taking notes and organizing them into a file. I made Pinterest boards full of parenting articles and projects to do with kids. I followed mom bloggers who gave "perfect mom" advice. I tried as hard as I could to match what I saw those internet moms doing.

The internet moms told me I needed to do enrichment activities with my son. Sensory bins and structured play. I also needed to read to him daily and take him on trips around town. I needed to make sure his plate was colorful and present him with healthy foods, even if he wouldn't eat them. I needed to have DIY craft birthday parties, and his room needed to have methodical toy organization. I needed to keep him on a strict routine, and I had to laminate and hang that routine in the hallway so we could check off the steps together. He needed age-appropriate chores and limited screen time. He needed cute outfits and styled hair. I needed everything to be done perfectly because my biggest fear was that I wasn't good enough to be his mom.

My son and I moved around a lot during the first couple years of his life: out of my mom's house, into a bad situation, back into my mom's house, and out again. I was a teenager trying to become an independent adult, failing, and trying again. I dropped out of high school, got my GED, and started college. I received state assistance and put my son in daycare. I got my CNA license and began working as a nursing assistant. I also started cleaning houses on my days off and brought my son with me, setting him up in a Pack 'n Play as I cleaned. We were always on the go.

A few years later, I met a man I loved and got married, which meant we moved again, into a new house. I started working full-time in a hospital. My son started preschool, and he started having frequent temper tantrums. I was trying to figure out the best way to handle them. It seemed like no matter what I tried, nothing worked. I couldn't even figure out what was causing these meltdowns, so I couldn't figure out how to prevent them.

I was reaching out for help and seeking advice. The answer I got engulfed me with guilt. I was told by a family member that my choices were causing him to feel unstable and act out. Because of the moving around and my new relationship, I hadn't provided him with a stable enough environment. With all the changes he was experiencing, of course, it was no surprise he was acting out this way. This made me feel like the worst mother in the world.

My choices and all my hard work—working endlessly to build a life for us and make sure he was in a safe environment— were being criticized and blamed for his behavior. I felt like a failure. I felt like I had failed my son.

At that time, I was twenty-one years old with a bachelor's degree and a full-time job saving kids' lives in a pediatric ER, living in a home I owned, married to a man who loved me and treated me wonderfully, and had a super smart, already reading, math-loving four-year-old who I loved more than life itself. Yet, I felt like a complete failure.

Reading that back makes me sad. To feel like a failure as a mom can feel like the ultimate failure as a person. Our identity can be entirely consumed by being a mother. So, if our parenting is criticized, that's like criticizing our entire identity. What are we if not a good mom? This is a heavy weight that a lot of us live under.

Remembering how I felt during that time makes me particularly sad for my younger self, especially now that my son is a wonderful teenager who I thoroughly enjoy being around. Today, I can see how ridiculous my fears were. Now that I am older and removed from the daily stress I was living in, I can clearly see that I was doing an amazing job. But in the thick of it, I couldn't see it. I wish I could go back and tell my younger self that I was doing a good job. I wish I could tell myself that things would get easier. But

I wasn't looking at it from a zoomed-out perspective. I was just looking at what was right in front of me, focused on all the ways I wasn't measuring up to the perfect expectation I had for myself.

The Need to Prove Our Worth

As I mentioned, in the depths of the everyday difficulties of raising small children, I always felt the need to prove myself. I started doing all the things I could think of that would make me a good enough mom. I became homeroom mom and planned elementary school events. I taught their Sunday school classes and led Wednesday night kids' church. I signed my kids up for every possible extracurricular that I could afford. And I completely burnt myself out and had no energy left at the end of the day. But what stressed me out the most were the birthday parties. All the moms online seemed to be competing for the best party planner award. When my son turned four, I threw him a pirate-themed party. I had a very limited budget but felt constant pressure to perform and prove my worth. I planned pirate games. I built a plank for the kids to walk on. I spent hours making decorations. I created a buried treasure scavenger hunt. I put days of work into that party. I wanted him to have a great time, but I also wanted respect and praise from the other moms in attendance.

Thinking back on this, I decided to ask my son, now sixteen, what his perception of that party was. I wondered if he thought back on how great a mom I was or how loved he felt because of all the work I did. But instead of a heartfelt response, he said he had no memory of the party whatsoever. *No memory whatsoever.*

I realized that so much of my stress about mothering was related to what others thought about me. I was drowning in proving my worth and the hardships of motherhood, but I thought they were the same thing. I couldn't clearly differentiate between what was a real mother issue and what was me trying to prove my worth.

Being a bad cook was one of my deepest mom guilts. I am terrible at coming up with meal ideas and even worse at making things that kids will actually eat. One of my go-to breakfasts became frozen blueberry waffles. My youngest son loved those. But I had so much guilt comparing myself to the other moms who made their kids hot, nutritious breakfasts. They got up earlier than I did. They sliced fruit, collected eggs from their chickens, stood over a stove, and designed animal-shaped pancakes.

I woke up late and threw a waffle in a toaster. I just knew I should be able to do better. My kids deserved a better breakfast-making mom. But I was struggling with trying to feed them the waffles, get them to school, and get myself to work on time. I beat myself up over this. The waffles became a sign of how badly I was doing. *I wasn't good enough.*

One Mother's Day, my son gifted me a piece of paper titled "All About My Mom." It was a cute little interview in which his preschool teacher asked him questions and wrote down his answers. I was reading through, laughing at how he thought I was ten years old and seven feet tall. But then I got to a question that made my heart melt. The question was, "How do you know your mom loves you?" and he said, "Because she makes me waffles."

Tears.

All that guilt. All that time tearing myself down and beating myself up. To me it was a failure; to my son it was love.

Added Pressure

There is enough stress when raising kids. The added pressure I allowed myself to feel took energy away from actual problems. The actual problems were things like their medical concerns or emotional issues they were struggling with. Most of the problems that consumed my mind were not real problems; they were problems I allowed to live inside my head. They had no actual impact on how my children were being raised or what kind of adults they would become. My kids felt loved, safe, and fed. The rest didn't matter.

We put too much pressure on ourselves. According to my grandma, this wasn't a thing fifty years ago. She raised small children in the 1960s through the 1980s. She says being a mom was much easier back then. She said it wasn't hard to keep rooms clean because the girls had one doll and a single pair of roller skates. She never knew what other moms were doing besides those she did life with. And those other moms were people who would help with the kids. There was no Instagram or Pinterest where you could compare kids' birthday parties. There were no mom groups on Facebook telling you you're doing it wrong. My grandma didn't worry about planning "enrichment activities." She says they went outside and enriched themselves.

Go outside and enrich yourselves. I started using that phrase with my kids, and it really worked. They went outside and found their own enrichment activities. Talking to my grandma about this was eye-opening. I decided to take a page from her parenting book, which made my life so much easier. Most of the pressures that were weighing on me, I had put on myself. I had to stop worrying about being the best possible mom and just take care of my kids. Live life. Focus on enjoying it.

Different Kids Need Different Moms

I quickly learned my kids didn't care about those "perfect mom" visions I had in my head. They didn't even know about them. They weren't worried about whether I was the homeroom mom who planned the party. They didn't care what food item I brought to the fundraiser. They just wanted me to show up. My kids didn't think about the other moms—the ones I constantly compared myself to and could never live up to—or have any idea what they were doing. They didn't need those moms. They just needed me.

Here's the thing. That mom you compare yourself to? She has her own kids. Her kids are human beings with their own thoughts, fears, dreams, and personalities. Your kids have those things too. But your kids are different from hers. They are different people. Your parenting style shouldn't be shaped around what other moms are doing. It should be shaped around your individual children.

You are your child's mom. You know what your kid needs better than anyone else does. It can be hard to figure out, for sure. But no one who is on the outside looking in loves your children the way you do. Those other moms giving advice don't know what is best for your child—because it's your child. What works for one does not work for all.

Different kids need different moms.

And we all have our own mom thing. We all struggle with some things and are amazing at other things. We aren't supposed to be the same. I'm not the baking mom, the soccer mom, or the always-knows-where-your-shoes-are kind

> **Your parenting style shouldn't be shaped around what other moms are doing. It should be shaped around your individual children.**

of mom. I'm the mom who fosters independence, discusses musicals, movies, and literature at length, and annoys my kids with cuddles and repeatedly telling them I love them.

There is no right way to be a mom.

Are your kids loved, in a safe environment, and fed?

If the answer to those three things is yes, the rest is small potatoes.

And you get to prepare those potatoes however you want. Because you are the mom.

Some think that to be a good mom you must devote 100 percent of your time to your kids. You must be a stay-at-home mom who homeschools them and never lets them eat sugar. Others think to be a good mom you must work outside the home to show your kids they aren't the center of the world. They should only go to the best of the best private schools to be prepared for college. Or they should only go to public school to be prepared for life. They must spend their free time doing extracurriculars like piano lessons and tennis. Or they shouldn't have too much structured time—they need free time for imagination and creativity. When taking other people's opinions into consideration, the range of what makes a good mom is broad.

So, which mom is the good mom? They are all good moms. But not because of the education they choose for their kids or the activities they sign them up for. If your child is loved, safe, and fed, they have a good mom. We simply need to be the mom our child needs.

You Can't Control Who Your Children Turn Out to Be

Parenting advice is not one-size-fits-all. You may be a child-development expert or an incredible teacher who is full of patience and has a foolproof parenting plan. But the thing is, raising children is raising people. Children are individuals with their own thoughts and feelings. No matter how great a job you do, how your child turns out is ultimately up to your child.

Could I have done things better? Absolutely. There is always room for improvement in every aspect of life. But if your children are loved, safe, and fed, you are doing enough. We will make mistakes, but it doesn't mean our kids are going to be ruined.

When I was young, my dad took his own life, and it caused us kids a lot of damage. In the aftermath of that, my mom did and said some terrible things. She was grieving, and to us kids, because she had completely changed, it felt in some ways like we had lost both parents.

But in those dark days, my mom came home each night. She kept us clothed and fed. She worked constantly and provided us with a home.

Years later, after working through her grief, she apologized to me for the things she had said and done. That apology meant everything to me.

Above all else, during those difficult days, we knew without a shadow of a doubt she loved us. I still know this. I know that even in our biggest fights, I could always go back home if I needed to. *Neither of my parents ruined us.*

My husband came from a very rough childhood. As a child, he and his mother were homeless. She struggled with alcohol addiction. My husband was passed around and sent to stay with his grandparents, and his relationship with his mom was strained for the rest of her life. But one thing I can say for sure is that she didn't screw him up. He is a loving, caring, generous, selfless man who goes to the ends of the earth for me and our children. There is nothing more important to him than family. He makes me feel safe and loved, and I love him for it. His mother's mistakes did not ruin him.

Sometimes, one set of parents will raise children who are totally different people. I have a friend who is the oldest of four kids. All four were raised in the same home with the same two parents. My friend became a teacher. Her brother became a doctor. Her baby sister became a dance instructor. Her other brother became addicted to meth, and they don't know where he is. They haven't heard from him in years. They don't even know if he is still alive.

Their parents raised all four kids the same way. But ultimately, their children took very different paths.

Despite their upbringing, each person makes their own choices and decides who they are going to be. So, just love your kids. Teach them what you can and train them in the way they should go. You can't control who they become. But you can keep them loved, safe, and fed.

Unsolicited Parenting Advice

I think that, overall, people mean well when they tell you how to parent. I just tell myself that they must have forgotten what it actually felt like to be surrounded by small children. Because more often than not, the helpful advice I am given just makes me feel worse about myself and the job I am doing. It makes me feel like I am running out of time and everything is falling apart around me. It's just like someone leaning in and saying, "You aren't doing a good enough job."

Here's some of the unsolicited advice I often hear.

"Just wait until they are older."

Please feel free to ignore this one if you hear it. Small kids are really difficult. Give yourself grace. My biggest regret from when my kids were toddlers is trying to have it all together and beating myself up for the mess and the stress.

Little kids are messy and stressful. It's the season you are in. Big kids are messy too, but it's not the same. The things that are hard when they are small get easier. So much easier. You can make a big kid clean something up. It may include eye rolling and lots of repeating yourself, but they can do it.

"Don't blink. You'll miss it."

If we had small children forever, we would go insane. Kids become more self-reliant as they grow, and that is a beautiful thing. You can only go so many years without sleeping. Of course you love your small children, and you think they are the most precious things to walk the earth. But you will also love them when they are older. It seems to be a societal norm to be upset when your kids turn into teens. But I am here to tell you, I have loved it. I would not trade the teenage years for the preschool years.

Older kids are amazing. They may have been cuter when they were small, but let me tell you about these older kids living in my house. The conversations we have now are so much better than anything I have ever experienced. Talking about the plotline of a TV show or what my teenager wants to do with his future. It gets deep and it gets interesting. They make me laugh. They are easy to travel with. They are just so much fun, and they can brush their own teeth, buckle their own seat belts, and wipe their own butts. It's incredible.

"It takes a village to raise a child."

Okay, are you offering your services for free? Because if not, what are you trying to tell me? As moms, we have times when we need to ask for help. And if you are lucky, you have people around to help. But a lot of us don't. We are so busy working and just surviving day-to-day.

When I broke my leg, we were desperate for help. It's sad how quickly we found out how few people would actually show up for us when we needed it. People I called best friends disappeared. Family members I thought I could count on seemed to forget I existed. But you also find out who you can count on. And for us, it was two women in my family who took turns stepping up. My husband had to work, and I was in bed, unable to feed a two-and-a-half-year-old. Those two women would take turns coming over to feed him and make sure we were situated.

But some of us don't live near family or don't have family who can step up in our time of need. If you're trying to do it all, you will need help. Because doing it all is impossible. You can't run a household while homeschooling during a pandemic, working full-time, and making Pinterest-worthy snacks. You can't do it all. And if you are trying, please take a break. You can only run on empty for so long before you break down.

> You can't do it all. And if you are trying, please take a break. You can only run on empty for so long before you break down.

But yeah, a village would make raising kids a lot easier.

I mean, imagine actually living in a village. I have a friend who kind of does. She lives on a church compound, and they all have roles in the community they have created. I know that may sound kind of strange, but it's actually really cool. She keeps chickens and provides chicken and eggs to their community. One mom takes all the kids to school and picks them up. They each have different roles to help each other out. That sounds really nice.

But most of us don't live like that. Some of us don't even talk to our neighbors. So, if you have no one to help, what do you do? You must let some things go. Strip it down to the bare minimum. What can you take off your plate? Some people might get mad at you, especially if you've signed up for something that you are backing out of now. But there are times in our lives when we need to show up for ourselves and our immediate families before we can show up for anyone else.

We can't do it all, and sadly, we don't all have a village. Your village might be the fast-food delivery guy or the person who puts the groceries in your trunk. You might not be able to take off work to chaperone the field trip. You may need to skip throwing a huge birthday party for your kids. Your kids might just have to wear dirty pants to school sometimes because your village laundry lady didn't show up again. If you have people you can ask to help, please do. But if you don't, realize your limitations and don't expect to be able to do everything a village can do.

"You only have eighteen summers with your kids."

Lies. I hate that sentence. Maybe that inspires someone somewhere, but it doesn't inspire me—it stresses me out. When I used to hear these "motivational quotes" that tell me to spend every moment of my kids' lives enjoying them, I ended up feeling anxious and drowning in mom guilt. Especially the summer thing. When I try to schedule out a whole summer, I can't, and I feel like a failure. I try to enjoy every moment of my kids' lives, but when they won't stop fighting over slime or who gets to hold the bigger stick, I think I am going insane.

What I remember most about my childhood is the time we spent together as a family, whether that was driving in the car or sitting in the living room or our backyard. We didn't have to do anything extravagant for me to feel loved or like I had great parents or was having a great summer. When I think back, my favorite summer memories are playing in the backyard with my little brother, swimming in my grandma's pool, and getting to pick out movies that my parents would watch with us on family movie nights.

Those parenting quotes aren't meant for me. I don't need help worrying about how fast my kids are growing up. I am very aware of it all on my own. This year, my baby is starting middle school. My oldest is starting his senior year of high school. Time does fly by, and each year seems to get faster. We all know this and experience it. Think back to your childhood. It went by fast, didn't it?

This summer seemed like a big one to me. Like the end of an era as my kids start what feels like big chapters in their lives. It makes me feel nostalgic and, if I think about it, maybe a little sad. But I don't want to spend my time with my kids feeling sad and wishing they wouldn't grow up. I'm trying to jump into this next stage of life excitedly. I'm trying to focus on all the great things to come. I am reminding myself that this isn't our last summer. We don't get just eighteen summers with our kids.

I don't know about you, but even though I am in my thirties, when my mom asks me or one of my siblings to go on vacation with her, we jump, especially if she is paying. I plan on having summers with my sons when they are adults too. Just because my son turns nineteen doesn't mean he won't be able to clear a week to go to the beach with me. I have a future savings goal of being able to take vacations with my adult sons, their wives, and my future grandchildren. It's going to be awesome.

I had a male coworker who was around the age of forty and said he still went to his mom's house at least once a week. I loved hearing that. The narrative is usually that moms lose their sons when they become adults. I asked him what it was that kept him going to his mom's. I was waiting for some nugget of wisdom I could hold on to. Something I could start practicing in my life that would keep my sons coming back around. Instead of telling me about how his mother nourished a relationship with him through adulthood, he said she had the football channel he didn't have. It can be as simple as that.

We don't lose our kids the day they turn eighteen. If you keep them loved, safe, and fed, they might come over weekly, even when they are forty.

I am not upset that my boys aren't small children anymore. They are doing what they are designed to do. They are growing up. As they get older, they get funnier. They develop their individual personalities, and they amaze me with what they can do. And what is the alternative to growing up? Not growing up.

So, instead of being sad when school starts, I am choosing to celebrate—that they are alive and thriving. Celebrate that I have survived motherhood so far. And celebrate that I get to watch my boys grow into young men.

Write This Down

- What kind of mom are you? Write down what you are good at. What individual characteristics do you have that separate you from the moms you see on Instagram? Different kids need different moms. What makes you different?

- Are you trying to accomplish what it takes a village to do? If you don't have a village, what are some things you could let go of? What are some things you could ask for help with? If you don't have anyone available to help, could you hire help? Can you order groceries online or have someone else do the shopping for you? Could you talk to another mom in the neighborhood and see if she would like to carpool so you both have days off from the school drop-off line?

5

You Don't Have to Clean the Way Your Mother Did

My mother always said, "The state of your home is a reflection of you." That sentence really sucked the life out of me as an adult. I want my house to be clean and organized. I want it to smell good. I want you to walk into my house and say, "Wow, your house is so cute and clean." Because deep down, I have this ingrained belief that my house is a reflection of myself. If my house is put together, I'm put together. If my house is a mess, I'm a mess. But that's simply not true.

There is truth in the fact that a messy house can make me feel anxious and overwhelmed while a clean house gives me a beautiful sense of peace. But tying my worth, mental health, and identity to the state of my house was an unhealthy place where I lived for years. I felt inadequate. I didn't want to get out of bed and face the mess out there. I just wanted to escape.

While raising small kids, I called my house a disaster on most days. Walking into my home brought me chaos and anxiety. I would see my kitchen sink overflowing with dishes, cluttered countertops, unopened bills, and toys and socks scattered across the floor. It all made me want to scream.

Then I would walk past the kids' bathroom on my way to escape it all and be hit with the smell of urine. I would peek in and see dirty clothes covering the floor, toothpaste all over the counter, and the bathroom trash overflowing. I wanted to cry, *This is exhausting! This entire house was spotless just a few days ago. It looks worse than it did before I spent seven hours on my day off cleaning it.* At that point, I would have rage growing inside me, and I felt the urge to do one of two things: yell at my family or escape to my bedroom.

My mom used to yell at us when she would get to that boiling point. I can understand her anger now, but I remember how bad it made me feel as a child. I have tried really hard not to yell at my kids. So, 99 percent of the time, I chose option two. Escape. I knew it would take all day to fix what my family had done to the house, and I didn't have the mental or physical energy to do it. Instead, I would lose myself in a book or TV series. I would leave and keep myself busy with work or the PTA. I would do anything to escape cleaning my house. The task of cleaning was just too overwhelming.

Maybe you don't yell at your family or retreat to your bedroom, but you can probably relate to that overwhelmed feeling. I work from home now. The kids are older and can pick up after themselves more, but those deep-rooted feelings of inadequacy when my house is a mess can still creep up if I let them. I had to practice using tools to overcome those feelings until I became proficient. I found some practical anti-perfectionist tips that helped me get through the messiest years. Let's go over them.

The Perspective Shift

If you grew up in a house like mine, your mom expected a certain level of cleanliness. Things had to be picked up, dusted, wiped down, sanitized, vacuumed, folded correctly, and decluttered. Everything had its place.

When I moved out on my own and became responsible for the entire house, her standards of cleaning were ingrained in me. I tried to balance a full-time job, two kids, and my mom's idea of clean. I believed every section of my house needed to be perfectly clean at all times. It needed to look like a picture in a magazine, especially if someone was coming over. As you can imagine, I struggled hard. I couldn't do it. I was emotional and angry, and I felt inadequate. I could barely get my son to school on time after working until 2:00 a.m. in the ER and having to get up for a 4:00 a.m. baby feeding.

There was no one in my house criticizing me or expecting me to do it all. These were expectations I was putting on myself from the way I was raised. I was criticizing myself every day. My husband could walk into the exact same disaster zone and sit down peacefully while I was having an emotional meltdown and tearing myself apart.

If I could talk to that younger version of myself, I would say, "Please stop trying so hard. Just focus on keeping your children alive. You are in your busiest season of life. Things will be easier in a couple of years. Stop worrying about the house and just enjoy your children and try to get some sleep." But I didn't have anyone telling me that. I had my mom's voice inside my head. To her credit, she never judged my mess when she came to my house, but the things she used to say about herself and our childhood home in her overwhelm were deep within me. I was talking to myself the way she had always talked to herself.

Comparing my house to those of the influencers who appeared to have their lives perfectly together made me feel even more anxious. No matter how hard I tried, I couldn't keep up with it. The harder I tried, the more overwhelmed and depressed I became.

The chaos I was living in became unmanageable. My son didn't have clean clothes for school. My scrubs were wadded up and wrinkled because I never hung them up. There were no clean bowls for cereal in the mornings. My son couldn't find his shoes, and I couldn't find my keys. We were late getting him to school. I was stressed. My son was stressed because I was stressed. I was sick and tired of starting every morning full of stress.

I had reached my breaking point. I screamed out something about being frustrated and how I just couldn't get my life together. My husband looked at me so confused. "Get your life together?" he asked. "What do you mean? You don't think you have a good life? Look at what we have and what we have accomplished. I don't know what you are talking about."

His perspective was very different from mine. I was focused on all the things I couldn't do, and he was focused on all the great things we had done. This was the perspective shift I needed.

Now I try to look at my messy house through the eyes of ninety-nine-year-old me. What would she see? This one is super easy for me to answer because I have an old picture from when I was twenty-three and my kids were very small. In the photo, they are sitting in the living room, and the entire floor is covered in toys. You wouldn't be able to walk through without stepping on something. I don't know why I took the picture because toy organization was one of my greatest frustrations in life. I never would have wanted anyone to see what that looked like.

I spent so much time stressing about toys. I bought shelves, organizers, and bins. I tried solution after solution to try to find the perfect answer to this toy problem we had. I would think I had figured it out, spend hours organizing the toys, and then a toddler would walk in and dump all the buckets out.

You know that horrible sound of a Lego bucket being dumped all over a clean living room? That haunted my dreams. Each time I heard the sound of toys falling from a bucket, my blood pressure would rise.

But now when I look back at that photo, I don't feel that stress. My blood pressure doesn't rise. I don't think about how I went to bed so many nights feeling like a failure because I was too tired to clean it up. Today, when I look at that photo, I am overwhelmed with joy. I think about how happy their faces were and how sweet and precious that time was.

These days, my kids don't even have toys. Toy storage is something that never crosses my mind. I don't feel regret about how I couldn't find the solution to perfectly organized toys. The only regret I feel is wasting time worrying about it.

When ninety-nine-year-old me looks at my messy house today, she won't see a failure. She will see how precious we all are. She will see the beauty in the mess. If she does remember that overflowing paperwork I need to deal with or the piles of laundry I am ignoring because I am writing this book, she will remember it as a picture of my life that she loves to look back on, and she'll think about how sweet and precious this time was. She won't beat me up over this mess. But she will be upset if I waste these years stressing out about it.

The state of your home doesn't define you. My house was so messy when my kids were little, but that didn't define who we were; it was just a season of busyness. If I were to describe the kind of person I was then, I wouldn't call myself a failure or say I didn't have my life together. Since I am removed from the daily stress and have worked my way out of perfectionism, I can see myself for what I was. I was a mom who was working hard and doing a great job.

The state of your home doesn't define you.

So, I have decided to take that advice from myself and let go of trying to make my house perfectly clean. I've learned how to say the words, "That's good enough."

A Good Enough Home

I used to constantly say, "I'm sorry my house is such a mess," whenever anyone dropped by. But I started saying that even if I thought my house was pretty clean because I had such a fear of judgment when it came to the state of my house. I didn't want anyone to think I was lazy or that I couldn't do it all. But living that way doesn't do any good for the person who is visiting your home. Most likely, their home looks the same as or worse than yours.

A mom from school stopped by my house to drop something off one day. My house was a wreck. I knew she was coming, but I had just gotten home from work, and I had no time to try to pick anything up. I let her inside and took the box she brought into the kitchen. She looked around at my mess. I knew deep down she was judging me.

But to my surprise, she let out a sigh and said, "Your house looks just like mine. You have no idea how much relief this gives me." We both laughed. My mess made her feel better about her own. If she had walked inside on a day my house was clean and I had said something like "Sorry about the mess," how would that have made her feel? Awful. She wouldn't have been able to relate to me. Pretending to be perfect wouldn't have given her any warm and fuzzy friend feelings. But when I was honest and vulnerable, she could relate. We were able to talk about our common struggles, and we grew to be good friends.

I bet you know the panic. Someone is on their way or knocking at the door and your house is a wreck. You start picking things up as fast as you can. Trying to pull the house together so no one knows the way you really live. Sound familiar?

I went to a baby shower recently, and the host asked us to please excuse the mess. She told us they had been renovating and it was a disaster zone. The house had absolutely nothing out of place. Not only was it extremely clean, but it was also decorated adorably for the shower. A garland of balloons draped the fireplace. Baby onesies hung over the windows. Platters of quiche and chocolate-covered strawberries were arranged on top of decorative tablecloths. A beautiful cake was in the center of the table. A ton of time had obviously gone into preparing for this party. But still the host said, "Excuse the mess." Did she really feel the need to apologize after spending all that time getting her house ready for this party? What do you think those words do to the guest coming in? What are those words for? I think we say them to make ourselves feel less judged by the person coming into our home.

I see this all the time on Instagram, and I've actually chosen to unfollow a few wonderful ladies just because they would be showing their new rug in the living room only to gasp at the fact that a dog toy was sitting on it. Then they would profusely apologize that we had to see the dog toy. Or someone would say something like "Oh my gosh. Johnny left his shoes by the front door again. Sorry my house is such a mess, y'all." I thought, *What? We leave our shoes by the door on purpose in my house.*

It left me feeling like I couldn't relate to these ladies one bit and like I wasn't good enough. I decided I didn't want to be that person to other people. I don't want to pretend like I have it all figured out, because I don't. My house is a hot mess right now as I write this. But the kids are playing outside, my husband is sitting next to me watching football, and I'm snuggled up by the fireplace writing to you. We are using this house exactly the way I meant for it to be used when I imagined us living here. So yeah, my son's underwear is on the floor, but my house is fulfilling its purpose. It's all about perspective.

Don't apologize for the house you have that is fulfilling its purpose. Allowing someone over when your house is a disaster is a true sign of friendship. Let's extend that gift to everyone. Pretending to be perfect by apologizing for the mess after cleaning your house is not helping anyone. Pretending to be perfect only hurts people. Showing your vulnerability helps people relate, feel normal, and want to be your friend.

My grandma always has a clean house. I mean, always. She wakes up around 5:00 a.m. and just starts moving. She washes her sheets on a strict schedule and makes her bed daily because she can't lie down at night unless she lies down in a clean, made bed. Every morning, she makes breakfast. She gardens. She cleans her pool. She paints a room with a new shade of paint. She sweeps the porch. She doesn't leave dishes in the sink because why would she? She always makes her house feel more and more homey. I am not the same. I want to be. Whenever I spend a few days there, I watch her closely. She never stops. It's just the way she is. Then, in the afternoon, she sits and reads a book. Until it's time to make dinner. It's like her nonstop circadian rhythm. She doesn't like to sit still. Sitting still is my favorite thing.

So I was surprised by a story my grandma shared with me one day. She was in her thirties, with kids at home, and she lived in a cute little house in California. Her sister Cathy decided to stop by with a friend to show off my grandma's new house. My great-aunt Cathy was proud of what my grandma had and wanted to share it. Cathy knocked on the door, and when my grandmother answered, she was instantly irritated. Cathy was stopping by unannounced with a stranger. My grandma had no time to prepare. The house was a mess. She spent the whole visit upset, wishing she had been warned so she would have had time to pick up.

My grandma says she still thinks back to that day and regrets focusing on the stress of someone seeing her messy house rather than focusing on spending time with her sister. She has built this wonderful home in the middle of nowhere, Oklahoma, for us all to come to and spend family time together. So now, when someone stops by, she puts down what she's doing, and she spends time with them.

Your home isn't perfect, and sometimes people will stop by. Hopefully they will announce themselves, but sometimes they won't. Take the advice from my grandma. Don't worry about the fact that the house doesn't meet those perfect standards of clean that you have created in your head. Just let however it is be good enough.

Your Home Has a Greater Purpose Than Being Clean

Your home is the place where you live. It has a purpose. The purpose is more than keeping it clean or making it magazine-worthy. My home is where I raise my children and grow my relationship with my husband. My home is where everything important in my life happens. It's where the people I love the most live. I want my house to serve me and my family. I want it to be comfortable and a place where my family wants to spend their time. I would rather have a house full of happy people tracking in dirt than an empty house ready for the cover of *Better Homes & Gardens*.

Take a step back and imagine your dream house. It can be whatever you want. Money isn't an object. Walk through that house in your mind. Think about your kitchen, living room, dining room, outdoor space, bedrooms. Imagine it all.

Now walk back through this house in your mind, but this time, instead of imagining the floor plan or the paint color or countertops, imagine what you will use each room for. We all live very different lives, and we live with different people, so you'll have to tailor this to meet your personal needs. What is your dream kitchen used for? Cooking huge meals for a large family? A place to gather? A place to teach your children to cook? What about the living room? A place to snuggle up with each other? A place to sit on the floor and play games? Do you have a room dedicated to reading or painting? How do you want to use your dream house?

When I think about mine, I imagine it as a place for us to love each other, spend time together, and make memories. What never crosses my mind while imagining what my home is used for is magazine photo shoots. Don't get me wrong, if a magazine ever approached me to take a picture of anything in my house, I would jump at the opportunity. I would spend every waking second cleaning that spot and making it picture-perfect before they arrived. I would probably have to ask my family to move out for a week so they didn't mess anything up. But that's not what I want *my life* to look like.

I want kids running through the house, making friends, doing homework, reading books, playing games. None of those things are clean and perfectly put. They are messy. The life I want is a messy one. Because messy is alive. When I realize what I want to use my house for, it makes it easier to focus more on *who* is in the house and less on *what* is in the house. When I remember that my living room is made for memory making, I worry less about my old stained couch and more about what board game we are playing tonight.

Perfectionism at home doesn't look the same for everyone. We are different people. Our families are all made up differently, and our homes serve us in different ways. If you struggle with the state of your home, I hope you can see that perfectionism may be the root of your problem. Stop believing the lies, and take simple actions to create a home that serves you. When you feel overwhelmed, focus on gratitude for what you have and look for signs of life that can make you smile.

You Don't Have to Clean the Way Your Mother Did

While I was trying to be perfect, I did a ton of research. I spent hours online looking for that perfect cleaning routine. I read articles and books. I watched YouTube videos. I downloaded cleaning charts and created my own. The cleaning routines I tried never worked. I couldn't stick to them. I kept researching. Everything I tried failed, but I thought someone out there had to have something that would work for my life. I spent months trying to figure out the best way to clean and organize my house instead of just getting up and cleaning something.

That was perfectionism. In my mind, when it was time to clean the house, I had to complete the task fully, to my mother's level of clean—that white-glove kind of clean. The "you could eat off the floor" kind of clean. But that is not reality.

The truth is, cleaning is never done. Sure, you can spend your weekend cleaning to my mother's standards. And if no one else lives with you, maybe it will stay that way. But that wasn't working for me. I couldn't keep up with the mess. So I had to try something else.

I came up with the "good enough" strategy. I started incredibly simple cleaning routines and only cleaned in ten-to-fifteen-minute increments. When the time was up, I was done. What I didn't get to didn't get done. And you know what happened when I didn't finish? My house became a lot cleaner than if I had done nothing.

Perfectionism told me that when my kitchen was a complete mess, I needed to spend at least two or three hours to get it spotless from top to bottom. If I didn't have two hours, I wouldn't start cleaning. Reality showed me that when my kitchen was a complete mess, I could choose to do fifteen minutes' worth of cleaning, and by the end of the fifteen minutes, I would feel so much better. The kitchen wasn't perfect, but it was cleaner. My anxiety would drop, I wasn't mad at my family anymore, and I could be at peace with my kitchen.

When I found myself overwhelmed with perfectionism, I would do nothing. If I didn't have the time or energy to do it the right way, I wouldn't do anything at all. But the truth is, doing a little something is always better than doing nothing. And after several ten-to-fifteen-minute sessions of a little something, I saw my perfectionism with cleaning start to melt away.

As I began to get a more relaxed relationship with cleaning, something amazing happened. My husband started helping more. He always helped out when I asked for help, but suddenly he was cleaning things without any prompting from me. I asked him what changed in him that made him want to help. He reminded me that I used to get upset with the way he cleaned. He said I wanted everything to be perfect and he couldn't meet my expectations, so he stopped trying. He would fold towels and I would tell him they weren't folded correctly, so he stopped wanting to fold towels. He knows now that I am not going to get on him for not cleaning something "the right way." Today, I will just be pleased that any amount of cleaning has been done. And he likes to please me, so he cleans. He actually cleans more than I do lately, which is a complete role reversal from the first ten years of our marriage. And it's amazing.

It's not perfect. But it's cleaner.

The "Good Enough" Strategy

When I don't want to do something, I tell myself to try it for fifteen minutes. It's like tricking my brain into being productive. It doesn't matter what it is. It could be answering emails, exercising, or going outside on a cold day. If I tell myself I can stop when the timer goes off, I can get myself to start. But a lot of times, once I have started and things start flowing, I'm not ready to stop when the timer goes off.

I started using the "good enough" strategy when I was too overwhelmed to start cleaning. Instead of hiding in bed, I would start a fifteen-minute timer and clean as much of the kitchen as I could in that time. When the timer dinged, I would usually still have a lot of work to do, but I would stop. If I had the energy, I would reset my timer and do fifteen minutes in another room. I could handle those tiny cleaning goals, which motivated me to keep going.

I became amazed with how much of a difference I could make in just fifteen minutes. If I had an hour, I would do a one-hour speed clean. Fifteen minutes each in the kitchen, then the living room, then the kids' bathroom, then my bathroom. It started to feel like a game in which I was trying to beat the clock. After sixty minutes of cleaning, my house felt completely presentable.

I changed my cleaning mindset from thinking I needed to finish all the cleaning to taking little steps toward clean. Sometimes I would do just five minutes here and ten minutes there. It became about progress instead of perfection. In my perfectionism, if I saw a piece of trash on the floor, instead of picking it up, I would tell myself that I didn't have time to clean the entire floor, and I would just leave the trash there until I had time to do it all. But with a "good enough" clean mindset, I would pick up the piece of trash and throw it away, even if I left behind dirt that was on the floor. With this new perspective, I realized that a dirty floor without a piece of trash is better than a dirty floor with trash. I made progress this way and felt better about my house and myself. Learning to be happy with a good enough clean changed my life for the better.

Dealing with the Clean People Who Criticize Your Mess

All of this might sound great in theory, but what do you do when you try this, and someone who comes over is still critical of your mess? Remember, this is your house. You and your family live here. It needs to be used for your family's benefit. It isn't your mom's house or your mother-in-law's house—or whoever is being critical.

You can try the tactics I listed in chapter 3 to respond to critical comments. You can choose to ignore the comment completely, or you might choose to say something like "Well, I'm doing the best I can. My kids are keeping me busy, but

I try really hard to do everything to the best of my ability." This will cause them to pause and think about how their criticism makes you feel.

I believe vulnerability is the way to go. It's what will unite us. It helps us lift each other up. It is what will make true friendships and community. But you must be guarded with your vulnerability. Because there are people out there who love to tear others down. And when they sense vulnerability, they will try to squash it. You need to feel confident in your home's purpose and be okay with living in a lived-in home and not in a scene from a magazine. Once you fully accept that and see the beauty in it, you can stand up for the lifestyle you are choosing. You are making the choice to focus on the people inside the home more than the organizational and cleanliness expectations of others.

Write This Down

- Imagine each room in your dream home. Write down what you want each room to be used for.
- Now write down the rooms in your current house and describe what they are used for. Compare that list to your dream-home list.
- What parts of your current home are acting like your dream home? Is there a way to incorporate dream-home goals into your current home?
- Think back to the messes in your house or your bedroom from ten, fifteen, or twenty years ago. How often do you sit around these days regretting those messes? Do you still beat yourself up because you didn't clean your room well enough when you were ten?

- Write down how ninety-nine-year-old you would describe your house today and what it is being used for. What parts will she miss?
- Adopt a "good enough" cleaning strategy. If cleaning overwhelms you, look at the "Good Enough" Speed Clean that follows. Try it and see how it makes you feel.

"Good Enough" Speed Clean

This is about moving fast—quickly, not efficiently. We are not moving things to clean underneath them. This is a surface clean for when we feel overwhelmed and don't know where to start. This is not a deep clean, and this is not a "clean until it's perfect" clean. It's a *good enough* clean.

Start in the Kitchen

- Set your timer for fifteen minutes.
- Throw away all trash that is on the kitchen counters.
- Put away all food and other items that are on the kitchen counters.
- Move all dirty dishes to the sink.
- Take a rag and cleaner and wipe down the counters.
- Unload the dishwasher.
- Spend the remainder of your time loading the dishwasher.
- STOP when the timer goes off, even if it isn't done.

Move to the Living Room

- Set your timer for fifteen minutes.
- Clear off the coffee table.

- Put the cushions back on the couch.
- Pick up all the kids' stuff, throw it in their bedrooms, and shut the doors.
- Pick up anything else that's on the floor and put it away, or take it to the room where it belongs. Just throw it in; don't start cleaning that room.
- STOP when the timer goes off, even if you aren't done.

Move to the Bathroom

- Set your timer for fifteen minutes.
- Pick up all the dirty clothes off the floor and shove them in the hamper.
- Wipe down the mirror.
- Clear off the counter.
- Wipe down the counter.
- Wipe down the toilet.
- Empty the trash.
- STOP when the timer goes off, even if you aren't done.

Now take the last fifteen minutes of this hour and relax. Or, if you must, you can go back and finish something that didn't get done.

6

You Can't Do It All,
but You Can Enjoy What You Do

Growing up, I wouldn't have dared call myself a perfectionist, because I thought a perfectionist was that girl in school who got straight As, made the cutest posters, and always had a clean and organized locker. I didn't strive to be valedictorian, my locker was a disaster, and my hair was usually in a messy bun. I couldn't have been a perfectionist because I wasn't perfect and I didn't want to be.

I was wrong about that. Perfectionism doesn't describe one particular way of life. It is an umbrella term that can show up in your life in a thousand different ways. I was a perfectionist because I was setting high standards for myself in certain areas of life and I would tear myself down when I couldn't meet those expectations.

I had expectations of how my adult life would look. I knew exactly what kind of mother and wife I would be. I dreamed about what my house would look like and how I would decorate it. I always struggled with cleaning, but I knew that when I had my own house one day, I would keep it spotless and organized. I had all these preconceived notions about what my life would look like before I ever started living it. In my eyes, those ideas were what life was supposed to be. So when things didn't turn out the way they looked in my head, I felt like I was failing because I wasn't living up to the expectations I had set.

I have an incredibly hard time keeping up with trying to balance marriage, kids, work, a home, pets, family, and friends. I actually kind of suck at it. After years of berating myself about my lack of ability to be the perfect woman, it turns out I can't do it all.

More times than I would like to admit, I have wanted to escape my life because I've felt overwhelmed by the mess or the chaos or the to-do list. It takes so much energy to be that perfect person living in the perfect house, and at times I have felt completely drained. I have struggled with a seriously messed-up mindset about being the person I expected myself to be and constantly searched for information to help me get my life together.

When I found something good, I would be overjoyed with the fact that I had just figured out life, and I would be motivated to live that perfect life for about a week. Then something would ruin my momentum. A kid would get sick, I would get home too late to do my evening cleaning routine, or I would be asked to pick up an extra shift. And then I would end up leaving the dishes in the sink. The laundry would pile up again, and I would forget to take a kid to soccer practice. This would cause me to spiral down into my dark, overwhelming hole of feeling like a failure.

Where Do These Expectations Come From?

When I thought more about these perfectionist expectations I had for myself, I began to wonder where they'd originated.

Why do I feel this way? Why do I expect to have a perfectly clean home when I live with three boys? Why do I think I have to wear this particular size of clothing? Why do I think I need to be the homeroom mom every single year of my kids' lives?

I know this isn't what God wants for me. He doesn't call me to have a perfect daily routine, a magazine-worthy home, and children who always have clean fingernails. He definitely doesn't call me to have emotional meltdowns when I feel like I can't live up to the perfectionist expectations I've placed on myself. So, where did these expectations come from? Why did I have them?

Who gave you the expectations you have for yourself? Was it your mother? Was it movies or magazines? Your house isn't beautiful enough because you don't have the wood floors HGTV told you that you should want? Was it the mean girls at school, or the mean women at work who made you feel like you didn't measure up? Did they have an expectation of what your life was supposed to look like that you adopted as truth?

Not all the expectations we have for our lives are bad. Some of my perfectionist expectations include organized drawers and closets, and that's not a bad thing. Those expectations probably originate from the viral videos I watch of women turning a chaotic closet into organizational heaven. It turns bad when I let the lack of organization make me feel bad about myself. When my overflowing linen closet makes me feel like a failure is when I need to take a step back and reevaluate.

What are your perfectionist expectations? Who gave them to you? Should that person or thing have the power to influence how you feel about yourself? Should that person or thing have the power to tell you how to live your life? Is that where your expectations for yourself should come from?

As a society, we have high praise and respect for the people who look like they are working the hardest. The busier they are, the more successful they must be. The more to admire. It seems like, today, a woman's success is measured by how busy her schedule is. I hear women always trying to one-up each other about who has more on their plate. It's some strange competition to see who sounds the most stressed out.

I aimed for first place in that competition. My stress level was exploding through the roof. When I first became a mother and a wife, I had the idea that I needed to fill up all my time with stuff. That if we weren't busy, someone would call me lazy. If we weren't busy, I would be a bad mom. If we weren't busy, I wasn't doing life right. Staying busy was also a way I avoided coping with loss.

Two months after my second son was born, my best friend died suddenly. Michael was basically my brother. We met when we were five years old, and he was my person. People often asked us if we were twins. We acted like twins. He became a part of my family, and we all loved him very much. He was the person I talked to about everything. Then, when we were both twenty-two years old, his sister called me one morning to let me know he had suddenly passed away. I found myself at one of the lowest points in my life.

This was my second big, life-changing loss, and I was still very postpartum. I had two small children and a relatively new job. This just wasn't a good time to fall apart. I needed to keep it together. So I kept myself busy. I had practice with this. Keeping myself busy had allowed me to keep going when my dad died. If I kept myself busy enough, I wouldn't have time to feel the pain.

Overscheduling myself didn't make me feel better though. In the moment, signing up for things felt good, but it was a different story when it came time to follow through. With such a packed schedule, I felt more out of control and unable to simply get through the day.

During this postpartum time, I was working part-time and being a stay-at-home mom part-time. I spent my days off from work dropping one kid off at school and caring for a baby all day. Then we would have sports practices, games, piano lessons, church, and Bible studies.

I fell deep into a busyness trap. I was homeroom mom. I signed up to chaperone every single field trip. When I went to church, they told me I should volunteer. I watched two-year-olds on Sundays and ended up leading an entire children's church program on Wednesday nights. I started a small group doing volunteer work in the community. I joined women's Bible studies. I climbed the clinical ladder at work. I was promoted to vice president of the PTA. We had flag football games, soccer games, piano recitals, and birthday parties. I was doing as much as I could, and *I was miserable*.

I was trying so hard to find purpose and self-worth and to fill some giant gaping hole inside me with good and helpful work. It wasn't working, so I felt like I should be doing more. It's like I was trying to fulfill myself with a full schedule. That schedule wore on me. And instead of realizing that the busyness was a problem, I thought I just hadn't found the right thing. I needed a new Bible study class. I needed to join a small group. I needed to volunteer more hours cutting out laminated shapes for my kids' teachers. I needed to keep adding to the list of things I could do to make myself feel like I had a greater purpose. But it still wasn't working. Instead of feeling like I was doing meaningful work, I felt burnt out, exhausted, and underappreciated. No matter what I tried, none of those things fulfilled me.

Doing Less

I used to spend hours researching how I should be scheduling my day. Even though I was busy, I always felt like I wasn't accomplishing enough. I knew I had to be doing something wrong and believed there must be a better way to structure my day. I spent my time seeking out time management experts, and I learned everything I could from them.

Here is what I learned: There is no right way to get through the day.

After trying and failing so many of the suggested daily routines, I figured out what actually worked: doing less.

When my son was finishing the fifth grade, I was vice president of the PTA, which meant I was basically working a part-time job at the elementary school, unpaid. I was in charge of Fifth Grade Day, a big celebration for the fifth graders before they moved on to middle school. But nothing was simple in the PTA. We had to have meetings about meetings. At our third meeting for Fifth Grade Day, all the ideas I had presented in the first two meetings were shut down. I was told I couldn't use any of the plans that had been discussed.

There is no right way to get through the day.

And that was it. I don't know what happened inside me at that meeting. But for some reason, that was the final straw. It was some push I didn't know I needed to get out of that miserable cycle of busyness that I had lost myself in.

So I quit. I walked out. I felt myself on the edge of a nervous breakdown. And it's possible that I did have a little bit of a breakdown because that year, we quit everything. I had felt like I was drowning, and I knew I needed time to breathe. I pulled my kids out of all their extracurricular activities. That school year, we quit all sports and all music classes outside of the school day. I quit being the homeroom mom. I stopped signing up to volunteer for things. I stopped coming early to events to set up and stopped staying late to clean up. I quit teaching classes at my church and just attended services instead. At work, I quit filling out the extra clinical-ladder paperwork and gave up that extra dollar an hour and title that said I was a high achiever. I quit everything except my job and my family.

I wish I would have quit sooner. With the ability to spend my days off from work at home, not volunteering myself to the school, I experienced alone time—real alone time—for the first time. I was able to find creativity in myself that I had squashed from being so busy. When I was able to spend the afternoons at home, without traveling to a class or sporting event every day, I was able to hang out with my kids and connect with them. Not only did it take away my stress, but it took away stress from my kids too. They spent less time in the car traveling to and from our activities and more time playing in the backyard, using their imaginations. They needed that playtime.

After quitting everything, we started spending more time together as a family. We didn't have Saturday soccer games, so we could go on spur-of-the-moment camping trips. I wasn't completely exhausted all the time, so we could go on a nature hike on a Tuesday afternoon.

With this life slowdown, my grief hit me like a ton of bricks. But I needed to work through that. I desperately needed to. The pain of losing those two men in my life never gets easier. That saying "Time heals all wounds" isn't something I believe in. But I do know that sadness is an emotion that needs to be felt. Good things grow around the grief. The pain and the loss never go away. But a good life can be built around them. I needed that slow time to focus on building that good life.

Am I Doing Enough? What Is Enough?

I was overdoing it. So I wrote down everything I had been doing and tried to find the things that fulfilled me. When it came to school volunteering, the part I loved was being at the school for my kids. Being there for their parties, trips, and events—not running those things. Setting up, being in charge of, and cleaning up after those events kept me away from my kids and made the whole thing stressful. There were plenty of moms looking for their turn to put together a Christmas party, so I gave it up.

I did that kind of analysis with every aspect of my life, and I came to a clarifying realization. When I looked back on my childhood and remembered all the good times about growing up, they were 100 percent all about family togetherness and laughter. It had nothing to do with specific activities. It was just having good times with my family that made me grow up to realize I had a safe, loving, wonderful upbringing.

That realization helped me let go of the pressures I had been putting on myself about all the things I needed to be doing for my kids. If we could be together and laugh, that was enough to raise them to remember their childhood as safe, loving, and wonderful. And ultimately, that's what I wanted for them.

Would ninety-nine-year-old me think back and say, "I am so happy that I spent so much time scheduling every minute of our day so we stayed incredibly busy! I'm so glad I sat in all those PTA meetings. I'm so happy I spent all that extra time at work. I'm so glad I spent each evening cleaning the house until it was spotless instead of spending those precious minutes with my kids. I'm so glad I was so dang busy all the time"? No. I don't think she would say any of that.

I want her to look back and say, "I am so happy I spent so much time with my family. I'm so glad I gave up all the things I didn't love so I could spend more time doing the things that made me happy. I'm so thankful I quit trying to prove myself to everyone. I'm so glad I decided to enjoy my life instead of trying to perfect it."

There will always be things out there for you to do—promotions to get, volunteer positions to fill, gifts to give, to-do list items to write down and check off. You could do a million more things than you are doing right now, but at what cost? When I shifted to an anti-perfectionist mindset, I realized that I don't have to get everything done right now. Those were deadlines I had given myself.

At the end of the day, will you be happy because you checked off the most tasks? Or will you be happy because you focused on what was important and spent your time enjoying life?

There is a season for busy. Like when you are reaching for a big goal or if you are in college, starting a business, or raising a family. There are plenty of things to keep us busy. But if you feel drained and burnt out, I encourage you to examine what you could cut out. What is necessary? What will you think back on and be happy you did? What will you think back on and wish you wouldn't have wasted your time with?

Imagine yourself five to ten years from now. Maybe you live in a new place. Maybe your life looks completely different. Maybe you have all new friends and coworkers. What would that version of you say about the things you are doing right now to keep yourself busy? Are you saying yes to things because you are trying to please people you won't know ten years from now? Would older you tell you to stop?

It is okay to tell people no. It is okay not to volunteer. It is okay to say you can't help. It is okay to take a year or two off and just do nothing but feed the kids. I'm not suggesting you quit everything at the same time like I did, but it's okay if you do. Being a mother, a daughter, a sister, a wife, a friend, a teacher, a student, a nurse—whatever you are—is enough.

Write down the most important things that you want to be or do for yourself and your family. Mine looks like this: I want to raise kids who know they are loved. I want them to grow into independent, responsible, God-loving, happy adults. I want to experience new and exciting things. I want to experience those things with my family. I want to grow old with my husband. I want to laugh and enjoy our time together.

These are the most important things to me. When I look at it like this, I realize my job—whatever it may be—is not the most important thing to me. The thing I want most out of my life is to experience it with my family and for us to laugh and love each other. When I think about that, I can clearly see what is important and what is not. It's easier to say no to things that won't help that dream come true.

Yours may look completely different. Maybe your dream is to excel intellectually and raise super highly educated kids. You are going to stay busy researching and educating. Maybe you want to enjoy your family by running marathons together or playing sports together. So maybe a life full of soccer practices and games is exactly what your family needs. Every person's dream will look different. It's supposed to. The things that drain me might be the things that give you life. Just like the things that give me life might be the things that drain you. Find the things that give *you* life. Cut out the things that drain you.

Making a To-Do List

We tend to think that as long as we keep moving and keep busy, we are being productive. We fill up our schedules to stay active. John Wooden famously said, "Never mistake activity for achievement."[1] And that's exactly what I had been doing. I thought as long as I was moving, I was achieving something. But all I was achieving was seeing how long I could balance six different plates in the air and then feeling shocked and confused when they all came crashing down.

Even after we cut out what we can, we can still have an overwhelming to-do list. Life is full of responsibilities, and part of being a grown-up is showing up and doing things we don't want to do. We can all find things to keep us busy. But there is a difference between being productive and being busy. I am a "make lists / write it down" kind of girl. When I have a million things rushing around my brain, I can calm the chaos by writing it all down on paper.

And when I say I write it down, I write it all down. I dump the entire contents of my brain onto the paper. When I can see everything I need to do all laid out in front of me, it seems manageable. I write down all the appointments I need to make, the bills I need to pay, the paperwork I need to turn in, the laundry I need to put away, the emails I need to write, the friend I need to reach out to, the gifts I need to wrap. But this sometimes leaves me with a ten-page to-do list. Ten pages of things to do is a lot.

> We can all find things to keep us busy. But there is a difference between being productive and being busy.

If I asked my husband to write a to-do list, I don't know if he would even come up with ten things. (I just texted him and asked, "What's on your to-do list right now?" He responded with one thing, and it was about marital relations, so I will spare you.) There is a definite difference between how I go through life and how he goes through life. And it's not that I do more than he does. My husband is very busy. He equally helps me with the kids. He cooks dinner more than I do. He totally sucks at putting his laundry in the hamper, but he makes the kids breakfast and gets them ready for school every morning. He does all the house projects I ask him to do. He fixes everything. He owns his own business and works nonstop, and he works super hard.

So, why isn't he overwhelmed with a million things to do swirling around in his mind? He doesn't put the pressure on himself that I do. He isn't thinking about this idea of what he needs to do to be a perfect person. His idea of "good enough" is providing for his family and spending time with us. And he's right. In my eyes, my husband is more than good enough. He is fantastic. When I realized that, I decided to get out of my own head and try to imagine what my husband would consider to be my "good enough." So I asked him. He said he just expects me to love him and love the kids. Why do I put such high pressure and expectations on myself when the people closest to me think my "good enough" is just loving them?

Top-Three List

You still have this huge to-do list. Ten pages of things that need to get done. So, how do you tackle ten pages of to-dos? Prioritize them. Most of the deadlines we have are self-imposed. What's really going to happen if the to-dos don't get done? What's the worst-case scenario?

Life shouldn't just be about checking things off a list. But I've been there. In nursing school, the to-do list took twenty hours of my day. The only reason it was not twenty-four was because our teachers told us we needed four hours of sleep to convert short-term memory into long-term memory. So I made sure I got four hours of sleep every night. But the amount of studying I had to do to get through nursing school consumed every free second of my day. It was intense. And it was a horrible way to live. I have never been so unhappy. Life has to be about more than just getting things done. I need fun and I need rest. We need other things besides productivity.

But we have things to do. Those kids have to get to the dentist, and we have to get to work, and our library books are overdue. So, how do we do it all?

We don't. We can't do it all.

Accept that. We must prioritize what needs to be done. Sounds like common sense, but it wasn't for me. I really thought I should have been able to do it all. It seemed like other people could. But they weren't doing it all. It just looked like they were.

I started writing down a top-three list every day. Instead of trying to get as much done as I could, I picked just three things. Whatever seemed like the most important things for the day. Before I started doing just the top three, I would create a long to-do list and never finish it. What wasn't done would just get moved to the next day. My list never got smaller that way. So I forced it to be small. Because the big secret is that I didn't have to do nearly as much as I thought I did.

Three things each day are enough. Three things feel manageable. They're achievable. Because they don't seem overwhelming, I almost always get them done and feel accomplished.

I know it sounds overly simple and like it won't actually work. You have too many things to do. Three isn't enough for one day. But if you are struggling with a to-do list, I encourage you to just try it. See how it makes you feel. Many times, it gets my momentum going, and I want to stay productive and end up doing more than three things. But if I tell myself I only have to do three things, I am more likely to actually get things done.

I started sharing this strategy on Instagram. I listed my top three for the day and then posted updates as I completed my tasks. A mom with a toddler told me that she hadn't been to the grocery store alone with her child in six months. She was living with anxiety and depression. Grocery shopping was too overwhelming for her, and she couldn't bring herself to do it. She started implementing the top-three list and said she slowly started to gain her life back. She messaged me the day she took her child to the grocery store. She said she felt less overwhelmed and was a happier version of herself.

During the holidays, another friend from Instagram reached out to let me know that while using the top-three list, she cut things out of her day that she used to believe were mandatory Christmas activities. Because she did this, she was able to sit around and enjoy the evening with her family. She described it as feeling more like Christmas than any of her planned activities ever had.

An important time of year for the top-three list is Christmastime. To-do lists get intense around Christmas. If we focus on trying to create the perfect holiday season, we can work so hard and leave ourselves completely exhausted. Suddenly, Christmas is over, and we never took time to enjoy it.

Make Room for What You Enjoy

I've heard that Corrie ten Boom once said, "If the devil cannot make us bad, he will make us busy." That sounds right to me. Overscheduling my life only brought negative things into it. I believed the lie that I could do it all, and every time I couldn't, I felt like a failure. The truth was that when I slowed down, my life had room for joy. When I gave up on being a perfect person who met all the expectations I had in my head, I started to become an easygoing person I enjoyed spending my alone time with.

In my perfectionism, I was trying to stick to a strict schedule and achieve as much as I possibly could. I thought productivity would bring me peace. But the overly productive days didn't bring me peace; they brought me exhaustion.

There is nothing about perfectionism that has ever brought me peace. Instead, I found peace and joy when I let go of my perfect expectations for myself. Once I quit all our extra, unnecessary stuff, I found myself with free time to learn about the things that I actually enjoy and make room for them in my life. Yes, it's true, my to-do lists are almost never finished, but at the end of my life, I think I will thank myself for leaving the lists behind and taking this time to enjoy what I have.

I don't like the hurried, stressed-out version of me. She's not fun to hang out with. You can ask my husband or my children. They'll agree. I want to be someone I would want to be friends with. I want to be the version of me who has time to connect with the people who matter, even when deadlines are approaching. I can do this by letting go of what I think I should be doing and understanding that doing less now is doing more for myself in the long run. We can't do it all, but we can enjoy what we do.

Write This Down

- Make a list of all the things that are keeping you busy. Can you remove anything from the list to make more time for yourself and your family?
- Create a top-three list. Stop trying to perfect your to-do list and daily routine. Just prioritize what is important today.
- If you are stressing about a task, ask yourself, *Is this something that needs to be done right now, or is this a self-imposed deadline? What if it happens tomorrow?*
- What are things you enjoy doing that you never have time for? What could you cut out this month to make room for this thing you enjoy?
- There is no right way to get through the day.

TRADE

PERFECTIONISM

FOR PEACE

7

Build Courage and Confidence

What am I trying to prove?

That's a deep question. Another deep question is *who* am I trying to prove it to?

You may not have some big moment you can pinpoint in your life, like a teen pregnancy, when you started feeling the need to prove yourself. But you can probably recognize little moments when you've felt the desire to prove that you were worthy of a job, relationship, or friendship.

If you are trying to prove yourself to someone, you are probably doing so to gain acceptance or respect. The big problem here is when you tie your self-acceptance and self-respect to the approval of others. Your desire to prove your worth to everyone else may stem from a lack of self-worth.

Self-Worth and Value

I was an adolescent, so I try not to beat myself up over the fact that I didn't have the confidence of a thirty-four-year-old while my self-worth was being squashed to nothing. But I really wish I would have had that.

All the voices surrounding me made me feel inadequate at best. But something deep inside me, probably that unexplainable love that a mother has for her child, told me I was making the right choice despite the naysayers. I knew in my gut that I should keep my son and that I could do it. But perfectionism had me spiraling because I believed any little mistake would prove them all right. And overachievement took over my life.

When I gave birth, I was attending a public high school for teen moms that had an on-site daycare. The plan was to put my son in that daycare and graduate high school. But when he was born, they informed me that they did not have a spot for him. I couldn't bring him to school with me.

I ended up dropping out of school halfway through my junior year. I got a minimum-wage job and my GED. That fall, I started community college—a full year before my peer group started college. They were all starting their senior year of high school. So, in my head, I turned it into some sort of competition. I decided that I needed to graduate with a bachelor's degree in exactly four years. Then I would be a college graduate before my old friends who hadn't gotten pregnant.

One of the biggest stereotypes applied to me as a teen mom was that I wouldn't finish school. I became obsessed with the idea of not only finishing school but doing it faster than I would have if I hadn't gotten pregnant. I was accepted into nursing school, which was insanely hard for me. I took spring and winter interim classes and a full load every summer to be able to graduate in four years. I knew that if I could graduate at twenty-one years old, people would respect me and take me seriously. They wouldn't question me anymore. I would be worthy.

I was overachieving because I thought it would prove something to myself and others. And in some ways, it helped. I learned I could do hard things, which built confidence in me and gave me ammunition when someone tried to insult me. But the pressure and stress I put on myself kind of counteracted that confidence. It also didn't help me feel like I had inherent value. Instead, my worth was being tied to what I could achieve.

I think I probably heard this example about inherent value at church camp one year, and it always stuck with me.

Imagine I am holding a crisp $100 bill.

Me: "Would you like this $100?"

You: "Yes, please, and thank you."

Imagine me crumpling the bill into a paper ball. I carefully pull it apart, back to its original shape, but now it's all wrinkled.

Me: "Do you still want this $100?"

You: "Yes, please, and thank you."

Imagine me crumpling it back up again. I throw it on the ground and stomp on it. I pick it back up and unfold it. It is creased, wrinkly, and kind of dirty now.

Me: "Do you still want this $100?"

You are probably annoyed with me, and you may want to use a pair of gloves, but you say, "Yes. I would like the $100."

Even when it's beat-up, wrinkled, and dirty, you will still want to take the money because that $100 bill still has its inherent value.

Not understanding your value as a person is a problem. Many of us were raised to believe that our worth is tied to our productivity or service. When I was growing up, it seemed like women's entire identities were built by serving others. I think part of the reason I went to nursing school was because I believed that a job dedicated to service would make me a more worthy person. But our worth does not depend on how productive we are.

You may be overachieving to try to prove your worth, or you could be avoiding achievement because you don't believe you are worthy enough to try. If you are doing either of those things, or fall somewhere in the middle, you must discover your worth, and that cannot be found in achievements or outside sources.

If you are a Christian, you already know your worth is found in Christ. You are a child of God. You are chosen, loved, redeemed, forgiven, and all the things God says you are. But if you are like me, knowing this doesn't instantly make you feel good about yourself. In fact, sometimes knowing these things and yet still feeling unworthy makes me feel like my relationship with Christ must not be good enough and that's just another thing I'm failing at, which makes me feel guilty and even more unworthy.

Anyone else? That can't just be me, right?

Reading that I was enough never made me feel like I was enough. I had to find a way to accept myself, love myself, and truly believe that I was who God said I was.

Be Your Own Big Sister

I have a little sister who I love deeply. I love her more than any other girl in this world. She is like a best friend, but it's different. It's more than that. She struggled with her confidence growing up. She was adorable and a great athlete. But kids were mean, and she took a lot of that to heart.

When talking to my little sister, I want to say, *Emily, you are amazing. You have gone through a lot of difficult times; we both have, together. But girl, we're still here. You are just starting out. Do not let these people at school get you down.*

They don't know you like I know you. You have the whole world at your feet, and you can do whatever you want to do. You are funny, you are full of joy, and if you just keep going, you will get there. Don't stop. Quit telling yourself you aren't smart enough; YOU ARE SMART ENOUGH. Don't be afraid to fail. Try and fail, over and over again, but don't quit trying.

I want nothing more than to be able to build her up and fill her with self-esteem. I want her to be able to see herself in the same way I see her. When she tells me about something a mean girl said, it's so easy for me to tell her that comment was ridiculous. That she is absolutely nothing that girl said. I know that to be true. But my knowing it is not her knowing it. While I could try my best to build her up—and believe me, I've given her plenty of speeches—ultimately, she has to do the work.

My big-sister love made me do some deep thinking one day. I realized that some of the things my sister said about herself were things I was saying about myself. Things like not being pretty enough or having a fear of being too annoying. It was so easy for me to dismiss this stuff when it came to my sister. She is an actual bright light who could improve the mood of a room by walking into it. There has never been a moment when I needed her to do anything to prove her worth to me. She is valuable to me just by existing. I love her just because she is my sister.

If she is valuable just by existing, doesn't that mean *I am too?* I need a big sister to talk some sense into me. But as the oldest child, I don't have one. So I decided to become my own big sister.

When I struggle with insecurity or start to tear myself apart, I mentally imagine a stop sign. Then I replace whatever I was saying with what my big sister would tell me. I know this sounds a little ridiculous, but it works. After practicing this for several months, I started hearing that big-sister voice more regularly. I started thinking about myself in a more loving and accepting way. I started seeing my own value.

People can tell you all kinds of things to try to build you up. But self-worth is yours. You have to build it. No one else can do it for you. People can say things that help or hurt, but if you are tying your worth to what other people say about you, good or bad, you are putting your worth in other people's opinions. Don't trust them to determine the way you should feel about yourself. Don't let other people tell you who you are. That's got to be all you.

> **Self-worth is yours. You have to build it. No one else can do it for you.**

Everyone Starts Badly

I passed my national nursing licensure exam, and I became a registered nurse. I wanted a big-girl job, and this was it. This was the thing that was going to make everyone respect me. I was going to feel worthy, and everything was going to be great. All my self-worth problems would be gone.

But becoming a nurse introduced a new level of imposter syndrome. If you haven't heard of this, it's the common feeling that you are a fraud in a position you have been appointed to. It's as if you are trying to fool everyone around you that you can do this thing you have signed up for, like being a nurse as a new grad with zero experience.

New grad nurses can't do a lot. We don't know what we are doing yet. While learning this, I gained a new set of insecurities. I felt like I wasn't smart enough. I wasn't organized enough. I felt completely unworthy. It turned out that this job, this external thing that I thought would fix my self-worth problems, made them worse.

But I stuck with it, and I learned a lot. After ten years of nursing, my whole belief system about skills and qualifications had completely changed. I had naively believed that professionals were always professional and that doctors, surgeons, and nurses always knew what they were doing. They don't.

Everyone is terrible when they start. All the best skills I witnessed were done correctly due to lots of practice. These people are always learning and improving their skills. I once witnessed a great surgeon watch a YouTube video of a surgical procedure as a refresher before going into the operating room because he hadn't done it in a long time. Highly skilled people aren't different from you and me. They are just normal people who keep practicing.

I think I missed the first fifty IVs I attempted. But by the end of year ten, I almost never missed an IV. In fact, I was the girl people called when they had an extremely hard time getting one. That wasn't because I was naturally born with the skill to start IVs. It's because I had ten years of practice.

At the beginning of my career, I had set high expectations for myself. I didn't want to mess up. Missing those first fifty IVs was incredibly embarrassing. But why in the world would I think I would just be able to start an IV? My expectations were way too high, and I needed to lower them. If I was ever going to do a good job, I needed to start by doing it badly and getting more practice.

Lowering your expectations can sound like a negative thing. But to me it isn't. To me, low expectations are freeing. With low expectations, I allow myself to suck at something and fail. If I let myself do that, it's the first step toward getting better.

You live and learn as you go. You gain confidence as you learn and try new things. With that naturally built confidence, it's easy to find self-love and build self-worth. If you are struggling with either of those, you may need to start by lowering your expectations.

Actively Work Toward Building Confidence

Confidence is an appreciation of your abilities, leading to an assurance in your decisions. Finding qualities that you are proud of and focusing on them. We've already determined that we don't need to be the best at everything. We aren't going for Olympic gold; we're just trying to enjoy our lives and be confident as we do it.

Do not rely on others to grow your confidence for you. When someone praises you, it can be a huge confidence booster. But when you grow your confidence on positive opinions, it will be easier for negative opinions to cut it down. Your confidence is directly linked to the way you feel about yourself. Find the things you love about yourself and actively work toward creating more things you love about yourself.

So often, we can easily think of all the things we are bad at: wrong choices we've made, places we have fallen short. Our mistakes are easily recalled. It's harder to think about all the ways we are awesome. All the best things about us can be forgotten.

What are you good at? Where in life do you feel confident? Maybe you have a long list, or maybe you can't think of anything. If you can't name one thing you feel confident about, it's okay. You're starting from the beginning. Let's get to work.

Make goals and meet them.

Making and meeting goals is a huge confidence builder. Whether it is big or small, making a goal, creating a plan to achieve it, and then actually sticking with it will show you just how much you can do. Goals don't have to be big things like starting a business or running a marathon. They can be as simple as drinking a glass of water every morning or working your way through a reading list. Just remember that a goal has an action plan, while a dream is just a nice thought.

The first time I really felt proud of myself for achieving something was when I became a certified nursing assistant. I had to find and apply to a CNA school, go to class for four weeks, then take a state-certified exam. This was a whole new world for me. I had no experience with any of it, and the whole thing scared me to death. I was shaking on my first day of class. But I showed up scared and did it. I was nineteen and became a CNA, and I remember feeling like I had really accomplished something. That experience grew my confidence. It helped me believe that I could continue to work in health care.

Gaining a skill is a great way to build confidence. Set a goal to learn a new skill. It can be anything—knitting, cooking, gardening, dancing, painting, or chess. If you don't see anything worth appreciating in your life, learn a skill that you'll enjoy. Just remember that you may be terrible at it for a while. But make it a goal. Work at it every week. Watch yourself get better at it over time. Confidence will follow.

Do scary things.

You don't need confidence to do something that scares you; you need courage. How many times have you decided not to do something because you were afraid? Maybe you believe you can't do something, but you don't really know because you have never actually tried. Or what about the fear that you will mess something up? You won't do it right, so you're just not going to do it at all. Does that sound familiar? It does to me. I've said that to myself many times. But our confidence grows when we do something that scares us and we live through it. We come out stronger on the other side.

Some of the scary things I've done include confronting a coworker who was talking about me behind my back, giving a speech at my best friend's funeral, taking my two small kids on a twelve-hour road trip by myself, and jumping off a Tarzan swing in Costa Rica. I was scared the entire time I did each of those things until I came out on the other side and realized that I had just done something I was once terrified to do. Facing those fears made me brave. With each fear I faced, it was a little bit easier to face the next one.

When we give in to fear, we miss out on life experiences. Fear will tell you that you can't do the hard, scary things, but chances are, you can. If you mess up, you mess up. You gain knowledge and experience when you do something badly.

Fail.

Failure sounds like a bad word. It isn't. When you start something new, you will probably not be great at it at first. You may fail, but many people fail when they first start. No one is born walking out of the womb. We stumble and fall and practice for months before we ever take our first step. Then we take a couple of steps and fall again. But we get back up because, as a baby learning to walk, all we care about is walking. Getting that step in. Staying focused. We aren't distracted by wondering if someone will make fun of us if we fall. We just try, fall, get back up, and try again. If we didn't, we would never learn how to walk.

When you stop trying to be great at something and just allow yourself to be a bad beginner, you can be confident in where you stand. You can be confident that you're ready to learn. So don't be afraid to suck at something. Don't be afraid to fail. You'll never get good at anything or enjoy something new if you don't start.

I have been sitting here trying to think of a specific story about a time that I failed at something, kept going, and got better. But everything I am good at is something I once failed at. When I started planning trips for clients, my emails were so unprofessional. It took years of trial and error to learn how to get better. When I started cooking for the first time, I caught a paper towel on fire and dropped it on the ground, burning the linoleum floor. I'm still working on cooking, but I can tell you that I am much better than when I started.

> **Don't be afraid to fail. You'll never get good at anything or enjoy something new if you don't start.**

Sometimes failure makes us want to run and hide from the things we are bad at. But if we stick with them, we will improve. The more things you try, the more you get those "I just did that" moments. Those moments grow your confidence.

You are learning about who you are when you learn what you can do. Without knowing who you are, you might start to believe what the people you feel insecure around think about you. When you build your confidence and self-worth, you will know who you really are despite what others say, and you'll feel less pressure to change the minds of those who don't understand you.

There are times when we fail at things because those things aren't actually for us. I have a long list of business ideas I have started and failed at. But each one led me to something else that got me to where I am today. In 2017, I opened a booth called Creek Grown at an antique store. It didn't make enough money to cover the rent, and it didn't last long. But when I opened that booth, I started an Instagram account to advertise it. When I closed the booth, I kept the Instagram account, and I began using it to talk about anti-perfectionism. Which eventually led me to write this book.

Failure is a great teacher and can lead you to doors you never would have found without trying something new.

So, go find something to try. Do it badly. Then try again.

Prioritize Experiences over Appearances

In our perfectionism, we want to be seen a certain way by people. We try to dress and act the part. This can cause incredible stress in our lives. Have you ever tried to take a family photo when no one would cooperate, and you just wanted to scream at the top of your lungs? I have. I used to make family photo day one of the most stressful days of the year. I would put all my time and effort into selecting the outfits and finding the photographer and the location just to have a child fall in the mud before a single photo was taken.

I wish I could go back and take the picture with the little boy in the muddy shirt instead of insisting on changing him into a clean outfit. But I was focused on the image I wanted to portray to the world.

Trying to keep up a certain appearance is trying to meet an expectation in your head. It's one of my biggest battles in perfectionism. When I prioritize experiences over appearances, it's like a light is suddenly turned on. It's giving myself permission to enjoy the moment instead of worrying about what it looks like or what other people may think about it.

Those three simple words, *experiences over appearances*, give me a peace that reminds me that I don't need to prove myself to anyone. I can just live my life the way I want to. Those words give me the confidence to spend more time focusing on making memories and less time stressing out about things that won't matter in the long run.

This takes practice. Next time you are overwhelmed because things aren't looking the way you want them to, pull up a mental image of a stop sign. Take your concerns about appearances and replace them with thoughts on how to enjoy this specific experience. The more you do this, the better you'll get at it. Trust me, you should see the pitiful effort I put into family photos today. But they are my favorite ones. These laid-back photo shoots show my kids' personalities. They show us for who we really are. I'm going to love looking back at these pictures much more than our forced photos with fake smiles.

With this practice of experiences over appearances, you'll find yourself growing more confident in showing up authentically. Your focus will shift from the image you are portraying to the life experiences you are building.

Practice this: Set your phone on a tripod or lean it against something. Open the camera and set it to video. Line your family up and have them look at the camera. Now, surprise them by telling a joke that you know will make them laugh. Go through the video you took, frame by frame, and take screenshots of the best faces. These authentic moments will be more precious to you than any planned and posed photo. Yes, the quality of the image may not be as good, but the quality of the memory is much better.

Know Your Principles

It's important to clearly know what you believe in. Not what everyone around you believes in, but what you actually believe to be right and true.

I tell my kids to decide today what they will do before the temptations in life arrive. Know now if they are going to choose to try drugs when they are offered. Because if they wait until they are offered to make the decision, that's when bad decisions are easily made. If they already know they won't try drugs when they are offered, it will be easier for them to decline.

That was advice that I needed throughout my twenties. I didn't have peer pressure temptation about drugs at that time, but I did face temptations. I was always tempted to gossip. I felt convicted and decided I didn't want to talk badly about people. It was a challenge for me. Gossiping was so easy to fall into. If I didn't tell myself that I wasn't going to gossip before the gossip was dropped in my lap, I was known to make coffee and make an entire day out of it.

But I decided to stop. I told myself that I wouldn't participate when gossip found me. I would shut it down. When a coworker asked me to dish out the latest news or started telling me rumors about a mutual friend, I was prepared. I had phrases ready to go, like "Well, have you talked to her about it?" to try to shift the conversation into a healthier place. I didn't have to make the decision in that moment; the decision had already been made.

Knowing where you stand helps you make confident decisions.

Shift Your Mindset and Decide Who You Are

My seventh-grade teacher, Mrs. Cegielski, once told us that the cool kids were only cool because we allowed them to be. Those were ideas we believed in our heads. If we didn't like who the cool kids were, all we had to do was change our mindset and consider someone else to be the cool kids. That blew my thirteen-year-old mind. I had never once considered it that way. I just believed the social hierarchy I was presented with.

I based my feelings and beliefs on the opinions of all the other kids around me. I didn't have to feel any certain way about those girls who made me feel like I wasn't good enough. In fact, I didn't even need to think about them. If I didn't fit in with them, I could decide that my friend group was just as cool, if not cooler. I got to decide who I was; I didn't have to play the part that my surroundings told me I should. And that really stuck with me.

I am glad I was taught this at an early age because there have been many times through adulthood when I have needed this mindset shift. Whether it be coworkers, church members, or moms at school, some people like to position themselves as better than others. We don't have to play along with their superiority game. We can change our mindset and remember that we get to decide who the "cool people" are.

We get to decide who we are too. As we work toward building our confidence, we learn about ourselves, and we get to make decisions. We get to decide to practice kindness. We get to decide what skills to build. We get to decide who our friends are. We can decide to stop reaching for perfection and be confident in our life.

Be Confident Because You Have Faith

Ephesians 3:12 says, "In him and through faith in him we may approach God with freedom and confidence."

It's through faith in God that we can have confidence. But that word *faith* is the hardest part of my relationship with Christ. I'm sure it's the real reason why I have struggled with perfectionism all along. I wholeheartedly believe in God and the Bible, and I have asked Jesus to be my Savior. But a lot of those nicely spoken, hopeful messages that seem to bring peace to people don't bring peace to me.

Peace is something I'm always praying for. Losing people I loved at such an early age has shaped the way I see life. I trust

God completely, but I trust that God will continue to allow me to experience hard times. Lord knows I have been blessed with good times, and I praise him for those. I have two healthy children, and I am beyond blessed. But I know more bad times are coming. In John 16:33, Jesus promises us trouble in this life. It's easy for me to sink into worst-case-scenario thinking and have an anxious heart. But Jesus said something that helps:

> Truly I tell you, if you have faith as small as a mustard seed, you can say to this mountain, "Move from here to there," and it will move. Nothing will be impossible for you. (Matt. 17:20)

The idea that I don't need big faith changed the way I felt. If just a tiny bit of faith is all I need, I can do that. I've started wearing one of those necklaces with a mustard seed inside. I don't know if you've seen the size of a mustard seed, but it's incredibly small. I definitely have more faith than the size of this tiny little seed. So, when I am not feeling confident, am full of anxiety, or am not believing I am who God says I am, I hold that mustard seed between my fingers and remind myself that this tiny amount of faith is all I need. I say a prayer asking for big faith and peace, and I swear, every time I ask, he gives it to me.

But I have to do that a lot.

We're working through it.

Who God Says You Are

- *You are valued.* "Indeed, the very hairs of your head are all numbered. Don't be afraid; you are worth more than many sparrows" (Luke 12:7).
- *You are loved.* "But because of his great love for us, God, who is rich in mercy, made us alive with Christ

even when we were dead in transgressions—it is by grace you have been saved" (Eph. 2:4–5).

- *You are accepted.* "Accept one another, then, just as Christ accepted you, in order to bring praise to God" (Rom. 15:7).
- *You are chosen.* "For we know, brothers and sisters loved by God, that he has chosen you" (1 Thess. 1:4).
- *You are heard.* "Evening, morning and noon I cry out in distress, and he hears my voice" (Ps. 55:17).
- *You are free.* "Through Christ Jesus the law of the Spirit who gives life has set you free from the law of sin and death" (Rom. 8:2).
- *You are saved by grace.* "For it is by grace you have been saved, through faith—and this is not from yourselves, it is the gift of God" (Eph. 2:8).
- *You have a friend.* "I no longer call you servants, because a servant does not know his master's business. Instead, I have called you friends, for everything that I learned from my Father I have made known to you" (John 15:15).
- *You are not abandoned.* "God has said, 'Never will I leave you; never will I forsake you'" (Heb. 13:5).

Write This Down

- Make a list of things you are good at, and save it as a note in your phone. Include the qualities about yourself that you admire. Reread it often.
- Write down one of the Scripture passages about who God says you are and tape it to your mirror. Read

that passage while you get ready in the morning and while you get ready for bed at night.

If you are having trouble coming up with qualities you admire about yourself, look over this list and circle the ones you see in yourself:

Accountability	Forgiveness	Punctuality
Acceptance	Generosity	Purpose
Ambition	Gentleness	Reasonability
Attentiveness	Gratitude	Reliability
Authenticity	Strong work ethic	Resiliency
Boldness	Honesty	Resourcefulness
Cheerfulness	Hospitality	Respectfulness
Compassion	Humility	Responsibility
Consistency	Imagination	Self-control
Contentment	Integrity	Sensitivity
Courage	Joyfulness	Strength
Creativity	Kindness	Thankfulness
Decisiveness	Knowledge	Thoroughness
Dependability	Leadership	Thoughtfulness
Determination	Love	Thriftiness
Devotion	Loyalty	Tolerance
Discretion	Nurture	Transparency
Endurance	Optimism	Understanding
Enthusiasm	Originality	Unity
Empathy	Passion	Vulnerability
Faithfulness	Perseverance	Wisdom
Flexibility	Prayerfulness	Wit

8

You Don't Have to
Have It All Figured Out

Should I have a third child? That is a question that haunted me for years. I had two young sons, and I didn't feel capable of taking care of a third. I was so exhausted already. I love my kids so deeply, and I love the idea of having a big family, but both of my pregnancies were really hard on me. I vomited so often that I had to be hospitalized and given IV fluids.

When my sons were born, I never would have traded my days with them, but those sleepless nights wrecked me. I was tired all the time. I wasn't sad when they started to get older because they started sleeping through the night and I gained a little bit of sanity with each extra hour of sleep. Sitting there with my two kids, the idea of getting pregnant and starting all over again sounded horrible to me. But instead of trusting that feeling and being okay with it, I tended to overthink it.

We overthink things sometimes. Some of us overthink things all the time. Overthinking stems from some form of anxiety. We are often worried we will make the wrong choice, and instead of just making a decision and going with it, we find ourselves stuck and unsure what to do.

Analysis Paralysis

Analysis paralysis is a super-fun phrase to describe over-thinking something so hard that the fear of making the wrong choice prevents you from making any choice at all. The analysis you are performing leaves you paralyzed. If you are prone to overthinking, this tendency can become a seri-ous problem that could hold you back in life. Something big like which career we should choose or something small like where to eat dinner tonight can cause some of us to make pros-and-cons lists until our fingers bleed. There is a real fear of making the wrong choice and living with the regret of that decision.

When I was overthinking whether to have a third child, the anxious voice inside me kept saying, *But what if a third baby is God's plan for your life?* I started guilting myself into thinking that I needed to consider having a third child because it could possibly be God's plan. I started reaching out for advice, asking other moms how they knew whether they should keep having kids. I never got any answers that helped. I didn't feel a calling to have another baby. In fact, I felt the opposite. I had a deep gut feeling that I shouldn't. But I couldn't stop worrying about whether or not that gut feeling was part of God's plan or if I was going to mess up the plan he had for me. It was a big life decision. I would pray and pray and ask God what to do, and I was met with silence. I couldn't hear God telling me anything.

The Wisdom to Decide

I grew up in church. From as far back as I can remember, I was taught that God had a plan for my life. I had a special God-given gift, and I needed to figure out what it was and follow the path that God had set out for me. While I think, for some, that brings hope and a sense of fulfillment, it paralyzed me.

I don't know if it was my limited understanding as a child or if I was taught incorrectly, but I misunderstood. When I was told that God had a plan for me, I thought that meant there was one very specific plan I needed to follow. A path that God had set out for me. It was my job to pray a whole lot to figure out what that path was. That was a lot of pressure.

I overthought every decision I made, afraid it would take me off the path I was supposed to be on. I believed I needed to have everything all figured out so I could live out my life's purpose. If I could just pray about it enough, God would tell me exactly what to do. As I got older and had big life decisions to make, I would pray about them, and I would hear nothing. *Am I supposed to take this job? Am I supposed to sell my house? Is it part of your plan for me to move to a new town?* I prayed, and all I would get in return was silence and confusion.

I was sitting in church one day, as a burnt-out nurse who felt like leaving health care wasn't an option, when the pastor started talking about God's plan. As you can imagine, this was a topic I hated. It always filled me with guilt whenever someone mentioned his plan because I didn't feel called to anything. I couldn't figure it out. But this pastor said something I had never heard before that completely changed my perspective.

153

He said that there wasn't just one perfect plan. Instead, I was given the wisdom to decide what to do.

The wisdom to decide? Me? Decide? As in, I get to *choose* what I do? God gave us free will, I knew that, but I never thought about the idea that he gave us the ability to choose what we do with our lives. I thought I had to wait for him to tell me.

So, what if it's not about finding the perfect path he has in mind for us but choosing a path and letting him lead us down it?

Living with the fear of making the "right" choice ultimately caused me to make no choices and live in a constant state of anxiety. I didn't know exactly what God had planned for me, but I knew a constant state of anxiety was not it. I quit focusing on trying to uncover the master plan and just started choosing things. I started praying for wisdom, and I started trusting my gut. It was freeing.

Making a Choice

At seventeen, I sat in a fast-food restaurant with my newborn son in his car seat next to me. I was meeting Jennie, one of my oldest friends, for lunch. I sat there distraught, sharing all my problems with her. I had just dropped out of high school and was about to take my GED test. I didn't know where to go from there.

I told Jennie, "I don't know what to do with my life, but I need to figure it out right now so I can support us."

She responded by asking, "Why don't you become a nurse?"

"Because I hate blood and stuff," I replied.

Without hesitation, she said, "It's a great way to always have a job and support you and your baby. So maybe you should just get over it."

154

Maybe I should just get over it? Okay. Those words may come off as rude to you, but it wasn't rude. It was incredibly motivational. I needed to do something with my life, and I had no interests. I had no skills. I had no plan. All I had was a baby and a job making seven dollars an hour. Getting over it and going to nursing school was a plan. At that time, I didn't realize what nursing school would entail. But I had a plan. I needed something to keep me moving so I wouldn't end up like some kind of teenage-mother stereotype. I wanted to create a good life for us.

I went on to work as an RN for ten years and hated it. It didn't fulfill me; it left me drained. But I don't regret making the choice to become a nurse. I needed that job then. I gained confidence and did some amazing work. It made me miserable most days, but it was a choice I made at a time when I needed to make a choice.

It's possible a different career would have led me to where I am today; there is no way to know. But I do know that a whole lot of good came out of choosing a job I didn't end up liking. I don't know if it was the "right choice" or if there could have been a better one, but I don't spend time thinking about that or regretting the choice I made. When I think back on that time, I'm just proud of myself for working so hard, choosing something, and following through with it.

> **This life is yours. You get to make your choices, and you don't have to have it all figured out.**

Jesus is concerned with who we are as people, not with our career choices. When Jesus does talk about jobs, it's telling people to leave them and follow him (see Matt. 4:18–22). I don't think your career needs to be the center of your calling. This life is yours. You get to make your choices, and you don't have to have it all figured out.

These choices we make, like where we live and what we do, ultimately aren't the important ones. Take this job, take that one. Move into this house, leave that neighborhood. That's not what matters most. What matters to Jesus is that you follow him.

When You Are Afraid to Mess Up

My mom hasn't redecorated her house in twenty years. I, on the other hand, haven't stopped redecorating and changing my entire style since I moved into my own home. I am constantly inspired by things I see online that make me want to redo one corner or another. My mom has a long list of things she would like to change, but she hasn't done any of it. I asked her why, and she told me she is afraid she will mess something up. She is afraid she will do it wrong and she won't like what she has done.

I get that. I have been afraid of those things too. It's a justifiable fear. I have done plenty of things to my home that turned out wrong. But if it's something I want, I have learned just to do it badly. I do it even though I am scared to mess up. Making mistakes takes courage. It isn't easy.

When it comes to our home, I like to hire my husband as my main contractor. It's cheap labor. I am always coming up with ideas and projects for him. It's one of those things he tolerates about me.

We like to do all our home renovations and projects ourselves, not because we love doing hard work but because we love to save money. Sometimes it's incredibly obvious we did it ourselves. We have screwed up a lot. But we figure it out. Mostly.

Neither of us could be confused for professionals; we are amateurs at best. Sometimes we do a lot of research before starting a project, and sometimes we just wing it. Either way, it works out and it's great, or it fails miserably and it's terrible. We just keep trying. The more we do, the better we get. Like everything in life, we must face those fears and keep practicing if we want to get better.

Several years ago, I painted our kitchen cabinets. It was my first time painting cabinets, so I did tons of research. I wanted to be sure I did everything right. It was miserable. I had a baby, so I hardly had time between breastfeeding sessions to do anything. But for about an hour a day when he took his afternoon nap, I would paint. I took all the doors off and laid them out across the floor. They ended up staying there for about a month. I followed the directions about painting and drying time and hardware. Finally, it was time to hang the doors back up.

I looked around at my newly painted kitchen, so proud of my hard work. A couple of days later, I opened a cabinet and paint from the frame came off onto the door. A huge section of paint just ripped off. I cried. I was so frustrated. I had worked so hard at this and tried to do everything right, but I had failed.

My husband came in to save the day. It was no big deal to him. He sanded the ripped-off section, repainted it, and stuck those cabinet bumpers onto the doors. When the cabinet door was shut, you couldn't tell there were any issues at all. But if you opened it and really looked at the spot he fixed, you could tell something had gone wrong, even though you had to really look at those details to find the flaw.

At first, I still wasn't happy. I didn't want any flaws. But with time, I forgot it was there. Later, whenever I did notice the flaw, instead of feeling annoyed with the situation, I was reminded how much I love my husband. He is always coming in to help me whenever I need it. That flaw turned into a sweet memory.

After working through a few projects together, my perspective began to change. I wanted a big dining room table, and my husband built one for us. It has a lot of flaws, but I love them. Those flaws are proof that this man loves us and built this table for our family. One day, after we are gone, this table will still have those signs of his love. I love our table. I'm still using it almost a decade later. What I once saw as flaws, I now see as character.

I began to look at my home renovation flaws this way. Once I realized that my home projects didn't have to be perfect, it gave me a sense of freedom to do more. Yes, there is a spot where I scratched the floor moving furniture, and I have painted kitchen cabinets a few more times since that first time without getting much better at it, but these are all signs of life. I'm calling the flaws "character," and I'm moving on.

Walk Through the Worst-Case Scenario

At some point, I knew I couldn't be a nurse forever. I wanted to find a way out, but I had no idea what to do. There was a hospital culture that made me believe leaving health care would be too big of a risk. The idea of giving up a career I had worked so hard for was just too scary. It was a good and stable job. I couldn't just give that up.

Instead of quitting, I started transferring to other floors in the hospital. I was hoping to find a different work environment I could be happy with. When that didn't work, I started picking up side jobs to explore other nursing-related fields. I became a PALS instructor and taught staff members about Pediatric Advanced Life Support. I became a clinical instructor at a local university, supervising college students during their pediatric nursing rotations. But none of those jobs brought me any joy.

Then one day, the idea of a totally different kind of job presented itself to me. I had a love of theme parks. I enjoyed spending my free time putting hours of research into planning a trip for my family. So when one of my friends posted a photo of taking her daughter to Disney World, I was so excited to talk to her about it. I couldn't wait to hear about all the fun they had.

Instead of hearing the magical stories I was expecting, she told me they had a horrible time. They had spent one day in Magic Kingdom and hated it. I was shocked. I started asking her questions and listing off the things that would be on my must-do list for a five-year-old girl. As I listed them, she kept saying they didn't see that. They didn't meet the princesses. They didn't ride those rides. They didn't watch the parade.

I felt upset. Disney World is expensive. I was so disappointed that they had spent that money, went in unprepared, and had this outcome. I knew this could have been a much better experience for them if I had just known they were going and had the opportunity to prepare them. That's how I found the motivation to become a travel planner.

This was always supposed to be a little hobby that brought me joy and hopefully would make me enough money to pay for a vacation for my family. It started slow, and I made about zero dollars for the first two years. But I loved it so much, and I didn't mind not making any money. But in year three of planning trips, I actually started getting paid. By year four, I was matching my nursing income and sometimes surpassing it. I started considering quitting my job as a nurse.

I was terrified to quit my main job. There was something deep inside me that made me believe that quitting that job would be a terrible mistake. Planning vacations would never be a stable income. How could I give up something I had invested so much time and energy into?

I shared my concerns with my husband. He was so logical about it, while I was so wrapped up in the fear of the unknown. He asked me to consider the worst-case scenario. What was the worst thing that could happen if I quit? After talking it through, I realized that the worst thing would be if travel planning suddenly failed. I wouldn't be making any money, and I would have to find another nursing job. After speaking it out loud, I realized how simple that sounded. If everything went wrong, I could just find another job.

I turned in my notice. Now I own my own travel agency and plan trips full-time. My work-from-home schedule has transformed our lives for the better. This was never my plan. It's one of those times I am reminded to be thankful that things didn't turn out the way I had expected them to. In my perfect vision of my life, I never would have imagined this. Will life look this way forever? I mean, I would love to say yes. But I have learned that I have no idea where life will take me. Things look so different today than they did ten years ago. Who knows where I will be in ten years? Not me.

If you are having a hard time making a choice, fearing the unknown will not help you make a logical decision. Imagine the worst-case scenario. Really think about it. What's the worst thing that can happen based on your choice? Sit with that bad thing for a minute. That bad outcome might not actually be as bad as you worked it up to be before you thought it through. After spending time imagining how you would cope with the worst-case scenario, you will have shifted your perspective, and you will be able to make a choice more logically.

There Is No Perfect Path

Life is made up of a collection of choices. And one choice can drastically change the outcome of where you are headed. But no matter how many good choices you make, you won't be guaranteed that happy ending you might be looking for. Things are going to be thrown at you, and you are going to have to duck and swerve, even if that means straying from the path you so carefully chose.

I was obsessed with trying to plan out my entire life. Having a plan gave me the sense of security I longed for. But there have been countless times when my husband and I have made a choice and started down a new path only for something to happen that completely changed everything. It's like a bridge exploding, leaving us at the end of a road, looking over a giant cliff. We have had to turn around and go back. When we think we know where we are going, something can happen that turns us in a completely different direction.

We know things don't always go according to plan, but do you really take that to heart? Because knowing this should help you not worry so much about finding that perfect path. Even if you do, it's not going to be the road you imagine. Don't try to live the perfect life; just live the life that works for you today and change it up accordingly.

If you are stuck trying to decide which way to go, the important thing is not to stop because you are afraid of going the wrong way. Just choose something. Choose a major, choose a job, choose a restaurant. Pick a direction, and go after it. If it leads to a dead end, you can turn around and try a different road. The more you try, the more wisdom you will gain. The wiser you are, the easier it will be to make your next choice. Take the pressure off. You have the option to change your mind, over and over and over again.

Making wrong choices will help you learn how to make the right ones. You don't have to get it all right every time. There is no one grading you. This is your life, and you only get to live it for a limited amount of time. So don't waste time standing at a fork in the road. Explore something.

Author Rainbow Rowell writes, "So, what if, instead of thinking about solving your whole life, you just think about adding additional good things. One at a time. Just let your pile of good things grow."[1]

> **Making wrong choices will help you learn how to make the right ones.**

What if instead of figuring it all out, you focused more on enjoying the life that's right in front of you? What if instead of trying to control where you're headed, you just collected good things along the way? As you know, most things in this life are out of our control. But if you really believe that, there is freedom in it. The idea that I don't need to control the situation or have it all figured out brings me so much life.

Today, instead of stressing about the things in the world that are out of your control and worrying about what tomorrow will bring, focus on enjoying your life and collecting the good things.

Let's Open the Bible for a Second

In Psalm 32:8, God says, "I will guide you along the best pathway for your life. I will advise you and watch over you" (NLT). What I didn't understand was that being guided by God isn't the same as just being told exactly what to do. If you don't hear the voice of God telling you which way to turn, just do what you believe to be right. Follow your gut feeling. Maybe that gut feeling is God. But keep praying about it, because he tells us he will guide us along the way. Stay open to hearing from him.

In 1 Kings 3, Solomon feels unprepared and unsure about how to take on his new role as king. I get that. On a much smaller scale, I have felt unprepared with a lot of roles that have been thrown at me. Solomon prays to God and asks him for wisdom. He asks him to give him a discerning heart so he'll be able to distinguish between right and wrong. Then God gives that to him.

Every day I pray for wisdom. That old-lady wisdom. Ninety-nine-year-old-me wisdom. When I am feeling sad or stressed or unsure which way to go, I take a step back and let older, wiser me tell me what to do. And normally she says, *Chill out. You won't even remember this thing you are worried about in a few years. Quit stressing, and enjoy those thirty-four-year-old knees while you have them.* If I make a choice now and it's the wrong one, it's okay because I am gaining life experience and becoming a wiser person. I will try again, and future me will be proud.

How to Be Wise

Pray for wisdom.

Consult ninety-nine-year-old you.

Hang out with an older, wiser person.

Explore things and learn things.

Write This Down

- Ask God for wisdom. Write down your prayer. I love to keep a prayer journal. It's a great way to go back and remember the things that were heavy on my

163

heart. It's easy to overlook all the ways God works in our lives. When you have your prayers written down, it's incredibly amazing to read back over them.

- Is there a choice you are struggling with right now? Write it down. Write down your worst-case scenario. What will happen if you make the wrong choice? What's the worst that can happen if you change your mind? What if you fail and have to go in a different direction?

9

Feel Your Sadness and Collect Your Good Things

Note: In the first section of this chapter, I recount details of my father's death by suicide. Sensitive readers, please read with care.

The worst thing someone ever said to me was "everything happens for a reason."

Two weeks before my thirteenth birthday, my dad committed suicide. Whenever I tell people who haven't lived through that, their reaction is almost always the same. In my experience, people tend to assume all suicides look alike. They want to know if he left a note or gave all his things away in the days before he took his own life. They want to know what the signs were. But suicide doesn't always look like that, and it isn't always a planned-out event like you might see in the movies.

My dad was a really good dad. He was always there for me while I was growing up. He went to my school events.

He chaperoned field trips. He made me snacks and told the best jokes. Everywhere we went, he knew people, and they were always happy and excited to see him. He was really funny and just an enjoyable person to be around. People were completely shocked when they heard the news about how he died. They wouldn't have ever guessed he would do something like that.

He worked the night shift as a police officer, and sometimes while he was working, I would sneak into bed with my mom at night. He would come home in the early morning hours, pick me up, and carry me back to my bed. I would pretend to be asleep each time he tucked me in. I loved that middle-of-the-night tuck-in. He made me feel safe.

From a little kid's perspective, my childhood was magical. I had two loving parents, a home with a backyard, a little brother, a little sister, a cat, and a dog. I had it all. As an adult looking back, I can see what wasn't normal. My dad dealt with depression. My parents fought. There were a lot of things happening that I couldn't see. But all I ever felt was safe and loved by both of my parents.

As I got older, my dad's sister died, then his mother died, and my parents began to fight more. I think he was struggling harder than ever before and, though I was unaware of it at the time, he had reached out for professional help and was prescribed antidepressants. What no one knew at the time was that he had decided to suddenly stop taking them. If you didn't know, you aren't supposed to just quit antidepressants. There can be negative side effects, like suicidal ideation.

We had recently moved to a new home with a second story. I was thrilled about this because my bedroom was upstairs, and I had my own bathroom, which was the best thing ever to happen to a twelve-year-old girl. I liked to pretend that I had my own apartment up there. It was 2003, a time when cell phones were becoming popular, but we didn't have them yet. We had two landline phones. One downstairs and one upstairs. Our downstairs phone had started to act weird. Sometimes when you pushed the on button, it wouldn't turn on right away. It needed to be replaced.

We were all at home the night my dad took his own life. It was a school night, and my brother and I had gone to bed. My sister was two, and she was still awake, standing in the kitchen with my mom. It wasn't too late because I was still awake listening to a CD when I heard a giant, loud crashing sound. We had a metal baker's rack in the kitchen. When I heard the sound, I immediately thought that the baker's rack had fallen over. I don't know why that was my first thought. But my brain needed to rationalize the sound, and the idea that it was a gunshot inside the house never would have crossed my mind.

With the crashing sound came the scream. My mom was screaming. But with that first scream, I assumed it was a star- tled reaction to the baker's rack falling over. My mom was known to have big, loud reactions. But then she screamed again. And then she screamed my sister's name. And then she screamed my dad's name over and over. That's when I got scared.

Because she was screaming for my dad, I believed someone must have broken into our house or something and she was screaming for his help. I heard her start running up the stairs. I sat up in my bed, listening to the footsteps and waiting for her to reach my room. She swung open my door with my sister in one arm and the downstairs phone in the other. She said the words "Dad just shot himself." She was in a panic. The downstairs phone wasn't turning on, so she came up to grab the upstairs phone. She handed my sister to me and ran back down the stairs calling 911.

She handed my sister to me. That's the moment my childhood ended. I took my sister into the bathroom and shut and locked the door. I pressed my back against it and held her against my chest. She was calm. She wasn't crying. I wasn't crying. We just stood there in silence.

I had one single tear roll down my face. I started praying. At that point, I still didn't believe my dad had killed himself. When my mom said that he had shot himself, I assumed it was an accidental gunshot. That he was getting ready for work and the gun must have gone off and he was shot in the leg. I remember telling God that I knew everything was going to be okay. I trusted him, and I knew he would keep my dad safe because he wouldn't let something bad like this happen to us. Nothing bad like this had ever happened before.

I could hear men in my house, police and paramedics. I decided to go downstairs to see what was going on. But as I reached the stairs, there was a man waiting there who told me to turn around and not come down. I went back into the bathroom. I don't have a clear memory of how long we waited or even how they got my attention that it was time to go. But I clearly remember holding my sister, being led down the stairs past men holding up a giant black tarp in my living room to obstruct my view of what was behind it.

They took us outside and put us in the back of the ambulance. There was only one ambulance at our house, and we were the last to get in. Inside, my brother was sleeping soundly through everything, completely unaware. My mom was lying down, hysterically crying, unable to form words. A paramedic turned to me and asked if there was someone to call. I gave them my aunt's number. The song "Ain't No Sunshine" by Bill Withers played on the radio. I knew that song, I liked that song. I focused on that song. Because I didn't want to focus on what I was thinking. I knew they wouldn't have put us in the ambulance if my dad was still alive.

No one told me, "Your dad died." No one really said anything to me at all that night. My aunt and uncle picked us up and put the three of us in their car. It was just us kids, alone for a minute, when my brother woke up. Our house was surrounded by police cars. He looked around at all the flashing lights and said, "Someone should call Dad," and then laid his head down and went back to sleep. My aunt and uncle drove us to my grandmother's house. My mom stayed behind in the ambulance.

There was no note. My dad hadn't been giving his stuff away. In fact, he had been prepping for a birthday camping trip for my little brother that weekend. He was turning nine. I don't believe he thought it through when he pulled out his gun. I don't know what he was thinking. He wasn't thinking about my two-year-old sister, who witnessed the horror. He wasn't thinking about my mom or the trauma this would cause. He wasn't thinking about my brother, who he would leave behind, fatherless. And he wasn't thinking about me.

One thing I know for sure is that my dad loved us. But I will never know why he did this. I can speculate about it— and trust me, I have. But to cope, I just have to believe he wasn't thinking at all. I have to believe he regretted it the moment he pulled the trigger.

When something like this happens, people don't know how to act. I don't blame them for that. I mostly remember people bringing food and looking at me with their sad faces. But the words "everything happens for a reason" were hurtful. I think that's one of the worst things you can say when someone is going through something terrible.

I don't believe it's true. Everything does not happen for a reason. People make terrible choices and do terrible things for no good reason at all. When that phrase is said, it's usually with good intentions, but it isn't helpful. It's not something people want to hear when they have just lost their job and don't know how to feed their family. Or if their infant passes away two hours after being born. Or if you're a nine-year-old boy whose father has just committed suicide. To the person suffering, it can be a very hurtful thing to say.

Those words filled me with rage when people said them to me. My dad killed himself for a reason? What reason? What reason could possibly be more important than my little brother and my baby sister growing up with a father? What could be more important than our family not being beaten down by tragedy? What reason justifies this?

There is no reason to justify what he did. He had a mental illness. He made a choice to take himself from this world, and he left us with the aftermath. What he did was horrible. It hurt us. It hurt his father. It hurt our community. According to my mom's therapist, it would lead to my rebellious behavior of using drugs and alcohol. It would lead to my brother's poor grades in school and my sister's separation anxiety. It certainly led to my mother's deep grief and inability to get out of bed. It wrecked us.

Grow Around Grief

People say time heals all wounds. But it had been decades and my wounds hadn't healed. Yes, I've carried on and kept living, but I still feel this deep sorrow when it comes to the dad-shaped hole in my life. Sometimes I would hear people describe their grief as something they had worked through, like it was something from the past, but with time they were able to move on. I wondered what was wrong with me. No matter how old I got, losing my dad never felt easier.

Twenty years after he died, I found an article written by Dr. Lois Tonkin titled "Growing Around Grief—Another Way of Looking at Grief and Recovery."[1] Her outlook on grief was what I had been searching for. It made sense of how I had been feeling over the last two decades and made me feel less like someone who just couldn't get over it and more like someone experiencing a normal form of grief.

In the article, grief is not described as a process with stages or a step-by-step program in which you can just check off items and move on. Instead, Tonkin describes grief as something that stays with you. She writes about a woman who sketched an image showing how she thought she would overcome her grief. The woman drew two circles. The first circle was completely filled in with the color gray. That represented the grief completely filling her life. The physical outline of the second circle stayed the same size, while the gray shrunk down to a tiny inner circle. That represented her belief that, with time, her grief would become smaller.

But that was not what happened. Next, she drew two more circles to describe what grief actually felt like. The first circle remained the same. It was completely filled in with the gray color of grief, but the second circle changed. That gray inner circle, representing grief, stayed the same size. It didn't shrink this time. Instead, the outline of the outer circle grew bigger around it. Her grief never felt smaller, but her life began to grow around it. She was able to live within the larger part of the circle, around the grief.

There are tons of different beautiful illustrations online in which people have used their artistic skill to depict this idea. I encourage you to look those up. I don't have a lot of freehand artistic skill, so I stuck to circles to illustrate this for myself.

expectation of grief

growing around grief

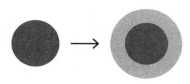

We live in an imperfect world where suffering is a part of life. I don't believe this tragedy was part of God's plan for our lives. I also don't believe that everything that happens to us is for some greater reason. Sometimes people make horrible choices that impact us. We can't control the loss and trauma we will endure.

One thing you can know for sure is that you are going to have hard times. If you aren't currently going through a hard time, you either recently went through one or your hard time is yet to come. Life is full of hard things. So, how do you find joy in a life full of suffering and hardship? You keep growing that outer circle around your grief.

Since my dad died, I've had two beautiful children. I married the love of my life. I have deepened my relationship with my mother and siblings. I've made friends. I've experienced incredible things. I've laughed a lot. I've wished my dad was here to witness it. I've wished he was here to be a grandpa for my kids. But the grief that still lives within me doesn't take away from the beautiful life I have grown.

Hard Times Can Work for Good

I do believe we can keep going and experience a beautiful life around our struggles. I also believe that bad things can work for good. In Romans 8:28, the apostle Paul writes, "And we know that in all things God works for the good of those who love him, who have been called according to his purpose." He doesn't say everything happens for a reason. But you can live through the hard times, and God can use them to work for good.

I wouldn't have believed that when I was a young teen in the depths of the despair of a completely broken family. Bible verses didn't feel helpful while I watched my entire world fall apart. I wouldn't have been able to think of anything good enough to justify the tragedy my family had endured. But that verse wasn't written as a justification. It was written as a truth for those who know God. Paul lists his struggles clearly for us in his second letter to the Corinthians:

I have worked harder, been put in prison more often, been whipped times without number, and faced death again and again. Five different times the Jewish leaders gave me thirty-nine lashes. Three times I was beaten with rods. Once I was stoned. Three times I was shipwrecked. Once I spent a whole night and a day adrift at sea. I have traveled on many long journeys. I have faced danger from rivers and from robbers. I have faced danger from my own people, the Jews, as well as from the Gentiles. I have faced danger in the cities, in the deserts, and on the seas. And I have faced danger from men who claim to be believers but are not. I have worked hard and long, enduring many sleepless nights. I have been hungry and thirsty and have often gone without food. I have shivered in the cold, without enough clothing to keep me warm. (2 Cor. 11:23–27 NLT)

I wish I would have read these verses after my dad died. I would have benefited more from hearing stories about hardship than the trivial mentions of "it's going to be okay" that I got. These are the kinds of verses that draw me in. Paul didn't have it easy, but he believed that all things would work together for good. As I got older, things started happening that made Romans 8:28 go from a nice saying to a verse that gave me a sense of peace.

I was twenty years old—eight years after my dad had taken his life—and in nursing school. I was taking a psych class and had to do my clinicals at a local psychiatric hospital. Our job was to go find our assigned patient and do a psychiatric assessment interview. Basically, a long conversation in which I asked a lot of personal questions. This wasn't my idea of a good time.

To be honest, the psychiatric hospital was kind of scary. We were told never to walk the halls alone. And we were warned to be very careful because the previous week, a patient had grabbed a nurse by her ponytail and yanked her to the ground in an attempt to sexually assault her. As you can imagine, that wasn't what I had had in mind when I decided to go to nursing school.

But I went in and found my patient, who was a six-foot-tall forty-year-old man who had checked himself in because he had planned to take his own life. I sat down next to him and started asking him my questions: "What's your name? Do you have any allergies? Are you having suicidal thoughts today?" You know, the typical things. He opened up easily and told me his story. I'll keep it private, but he had a difficult life. He finished by telling me that his ex-wife wasn't letting him see his kids and that had been his final straw. He'd had suicidal thoughts for years but never an actual plan. He had gotten in his car and come up with a plan on how to end his life. He was driving his car, fully intent on following through, when he decided to check himself into the hospital to see if anything could change his mind.

I asked him if any of the therapy was working, and he looked at me, paused for what felt like an incredibly long time, and said, "No. Not at all. It's all the same things I have heard before. But I can't tell them that or they won't let me out of here." Then something came over me, and I began wanting to talk to this man as a friend instead of a professional nursing student. I knew I wasn't supposed to. I wasn't there to give advice or share my story. I was there to do a job and learn the clinical side of nursing care. I started slowly by asking him what he thought would happen to the people he was leaving behind if he did take his life. He responded by saying he thought they would be fine. They didn't need him now, so they wouldn't miss him later.

At that point, I couldn't help myself. It just fell out of my mouth. I told him the story of my dad. It was a short version of the story, just a few sentences. I wasn't judging him. I wasn't shaming him. I was just simply, unemotionally telling him what my dad did. I told him it was right before my thirteenth birthday. I told him we never saw it coming. I told him it rocked me to my core, and I still dealt with a sense of abandonment and grief years later.

This six-foot-tall man was sitting there in his chair with tears streaking his face. He looked at me and said, "Thank you for telling me that. I think I came here for a reason, and I think that reason was to hear your story. I don't want my daughter to feel like I abandoned her." I left that conversation thinking that maybe my pain actually would work toward something good. Maybe I'll be able to see that good, maybe I won't. If I could go back and change things so that my dad didn't take his life, I would in a heartbeat. But I can't do that, so maybe I can find some peace knowing what happened will work for good.

I usually share this story on social media in November, in remembrance of the day my dad left us. I have a photo of the two of us that I love so much. I am two or three, and he's carrying me. It's candid and feels like an actual captured moment when I was purely innocent and safe and loved. I like to post that photo and share words about grief because losing my dad is still something that's very hard for me. I hope I can encourage others to know that if they are still struggling years after a loss, they are not alone. If the grief checklist didn't work for them either, I want them to know I understand them.

What I didn't imagine would happen were the messages I received from moms with young kids at home. I had moms thanking me for sharing my story because they had considered taking their own lives. They didn't believe that their children needed them. Hearing my story helped them realize the pain they would cause their children if they made that choice. They didn't want their children to feel the pain I had felt.

Reading those stories makes my jaw drop every time. When I share my story, I imagine a grieving person relating to me and feeling hope about growing life around their grief; I never imagined that my pain could possibly stop another child from losing their parent in the same way. I never considered my pain could work for good in another child's life.

We Need to Feel Our Sadness

We cannot be happy all the time. There is a time for happiness and there is a time for sadness. The Bible says there is "a time to weep and a time to laugh, a time to mourn and a time to dance" (Eccles. 3:4). *We are supposed to feel it all.* When bad things are bad, we need to weep. We need to mourn. We aren't supposed to just swallow the bad feelings and keep them down, like I tried to do for years.

After my dad died, my mom . . . she fell apart. She was thirty-six years old when she witnessed her husband commit suicide. I am almost that age now and can't even imagine. I don't blame her for how she processed her grief, but it was hard on me. She was not the mother I knew after that. She wouldn't act like the mother I recognized for over ten years. We had lost our dad, but in a way, we had lost our mom too. She was breaking down and falling apart, and it signaled something in me that made me feel like I had to hold it all together.

Deep down, I sometimes still feel like that. I have to be the strong one. I have to be the one who keeps things moving. I cannot fall apart. I have to remind myself that this isn't true. I have to remind myself that I need to stop and feel the bad feelings because it feels good on the other side of working through them. When I am trying to be tough and hold it together, I start to feel like I could break at any moment. When I take the time to cry and work through the feelings, I feel stronger.

> I have to remind myself that I need to stop and feel the bad feelings because it feels good on the other side of working through them.

Last year, I was numb. I was pushing everything down; I wasn't dealing with my pain. I could tell there was a problem, and every day it was getting worse. I read articles on how to fight depression. I went for walks, I would sing, I would dance, I would drown myself in television. I would scroll social media for hours. I would distract myself all day and night to keep myself from feeling sad.

But sadness is a part of life. Some things are too big to "positivity chant" away. Some things need to be worked through. There is a time for sadness. And after you have spent time in sadness, there is a time to rise out of it. There is a time to choose to stand back up, to choose to live for what you still have, to find things to be thankful for, and to continue to grow your life around your grief.

A few years ago, in the middle of trying to keep myself too busy to hear my own thoughts, I was shocked at what finally caused me to break. I think it had been two or three years since the last time I had cried. I was feeling really bad all the time. I had started online therapy again. I was reaching out to friends and family to try to talk about my feelings. I was struggling with just getting through my day.

My youngest child asked me to watch a movie with him. I hadn't seen this one. We made popcorn, and I cuddled up next to him. It was *The One and Only Ivan*, a story about a gorilla who was kept in captivity inside a shopping mall. He takes a baby elephant under his wing and—*spoiler alert*—at the end of the movie, he is released into a gorilla enclosure at the zoo. This is a much better living situation. He hadn't been outside most of his life. This would have been like heaven for him. He climbs up to the top of a tree and sees that the baby elephant is joining a group of elephants in their enclosure. Tears started falling down my face.

This movie is a combination of live-action and CGI, but it is based on a true story. I couldn't believe I was crying. I didn't cry easily. My son didn't notice. But then, when the credits started rolling, they showed actual footage of the real gorilla being released into the zoo. I lost it. I started ugly crying. I was making sounds, and it wasn't pretty. I was laughing along with the tears because I couldn't believe this gorilla made me cry.

When my dad died, I cried once in the bathroom. I went years without crying over his death. But this gorilla got me. My son looked at me like there was something wrong with me. I felt like I needed to assure him that I was okay. I laughed and said it just made me so happy that he got a happy ending. But I don't think I was really crying about a gorilla. I think he triggered years of pent-up emotions that needed to come out. The next day, I felt like a different person. Crying had been therapeutic. I had just spent the past several weeks worried about my mental state. One gorilla movie, and I felt as good as ever.

We need to feel our sadness. We need to cry. It is a part of life.

Take the Time to Pray

My prayers tend to be quick. They're usually when I have a thought of gratitude or a request I would like granted. *Lord, thank you for my children. Lord, please let him pass his driver's test.* More often than not, my prayers are short little one-liners. I usually don't spend any time listening in stillness after sending out my prayer. When Jesus would pray, he would go out into the wilderness. He would find desolate places. He wasn't rushing through it. He spent alone time with God. We can't always run out into the wilderness, but we can be intentional with our prayers and allow for quiet alone time to actually listen.

I was in church when our pastor asked everyone to take a few minutes to silently pray. He said, "Normally we pray for what we want. But when was the last time you prayed, asking God what he would have for you?" He asked us to simply pray the words "God, what would you have for me?"

I tried it. Because why not? I had never heard the voice of God. It was something I had searched for, but I could never hear anything. I always felt silence when I asked God what I should do or why he wasn't intervening in my hard times. In church that day, I asked God, *What would you have for me?* I heard nothing. But because everyone around me was silently praying, I decided to ask again. *What would you have for me?* Silence. I asked again and again, focusing on the question.

After about a minute or so of repeating myself to God, something happened. I had a visual image of darkness filling my body—*a good darkness*. It was as if all the noise, worries, and anxious thoughts left me and were replaced with calm. In that moment, the word *peace* entered my mind—quietly, like a whisper. It was as if a wave of dark peace washed over me and soothed my soul. I think God was telling me that what he wants for me is peace.

That same pastor preached later about trusting God with our hard times. He discussed the question most of us have asked: *Where were you, God?* He asked us to do the silent prayer thing again. He told us to think of our hardest moment and ask God where he was during that time. I closed my eyes and bowed my head and asked God, *Where were you when my dad left us?* I didn't get an immediate answer, so I asked again. The second time I asked, my brain was filled with a mental image of being back in that bathroom, holding my sister. But this time, Jesus was standing there, and he was wrapping his arms around us, holding us.

It felt like God was letting me know that he has been with me the whole time. It gave me a comfort I had never felt before. I only began to feel this peace and comfort when I took the time to sit quietly in prayer. I didn't have to escape to the wilderness to be alone with God, but I did have to be intentional about my time in prayer.

Life Is Full of Emotions

There is a very real time for sadness and grief; they are important emotions. But even in my sadness and grief, I have this underlying joy. It's not a happiness that I can just pull out to fix my mood when I feel at my worst. It's like a hope that keeps me going. Even if I can't move right now, even if I can't get out of bed today, it's this hope, this inner joy, that reminds me that I will get out of bed another day.

There is a difference between having this inner joy and feeling happy. Happiness is an emotion, and emotions are fleeting. They come and go quickly. They are based on our surroundings. You could watch a sad movie, cry your eyes out, and feel overwhelming sadness. A few minutes later, you could go check the mail and find a huge bonus check you weren't expecting from your boss. Suddenly, your sadness is gone and you are happy. Not only happy—ecstatic. But that happiness will only last for so long. Something will come along to make you feel angry, sad, jealous, frustrated, or scared. Emotions are fleeting. They don't last.

> **Having a deeper sense of joy, a sense of peace, will triumph over any fleeting emotion.**

Your emotions don't define you. You can be clinically depressed and still laugh. You can be living your best life and still grieve. Focusing on being happy all the time isn't realistic, and it isn't the most important thing. Having a deeper sense of joy, a sense of peace, will triumph over any fleeting emotion.

What is this inner joy? It's an understanding I have deep inside that keeps me going. No matter what happens, even when tragedy strikes, underneath my grief and sadness is an understanding that I am going to be okay. It is an inner strength. It comes from my relationship with Jesus.

181

Life is not just a series of happy moments. There will be pain. The people I have lost helped me shift my perspective. I have a real sense of the idea that life is not a guarantee. I am very aware that any day could be my last. It could also be the last day for the people I love the most. My hardest times have given me this perspective that makes me want to prioritize enjoying life.

If you look over the timeline of your life, there will be ups and downs, good times and bad. This is something we all experience. It's a part of living. In between the hard times are beautiful ones. If we lived a life with only good times, the good times would get old and they would stop feeling so good. Like when you find a food you love and you eat it so often, it's not good anymore. The mundane times and the bad times make the good times feel set apart.

We're only here for a moment. I don't want to waste that time trying to be perfect or doing things that don't matter to me to try to fit in or please other people. I want to enjoy this life. I want to grow a beautiful life and collect as many good things as I can along the way.

I want those good times. To have them means I will have to have bad times too. This is life, and I want to fully live it.

What if fully living means experiencing all the emotions? Not just the good ones. There is grief and suffering and sadness. There is also beauty and wonder and love. We can have them all.

Write This Down

- Draw a timeline of your life. Start by drawing a horizontal line across the paper. In chronological order, write down the best parts of your life above the line and the hardest times below it.

- Look over this sketch of your life. How have these moments, the best and the hardest, shaped who you are today?
- How could some of your hard times be used for good?
- Read over your hard moments and find the hardest one. If you ever wondered where God was during that time, take a few minutes to ask him where he was. Find a quiet place and ask him over and over again, focusing on the question. Allow time for his answer.

FINAL THOUGHTS ON BEING IMPERFECT

You only get one life, and you're trying to do it right. You want to be the best you can be for your family. You want to be happy, and you don't want to have regrets. The fear of doing it wrong can feel like a lot of pressure. You just want things to be good. You just want life to go the way you think it should.

What if trying to live the perfect life is keeping you from living a great one?

If you take one thing from this book, let it be to remember to look at your life from a different perspective. The perspective you currently have is not the only way to look at the situation. Look at your life through the eyes of ninety-nine-year-old you. Check in with that version of you regularly. Let older, wiser you shift your perspective.

Living my life with this older, wiser point of view impacts how I choose to spend my days. It impacts all those little moments. When you collect all those mundane, insignificant moments, you end up with a whole life.

I want to remember that a messy house does not mean I am failing. The dirt tracked over the floor means someone I love came home. These little stressors are signs of memories I am collecting. Those memories will bring me peace when I look back on them.

I want to have an attitude of adventure and joy. I want to remember gratitude over stress. I'm going to seek out the good in the flaws. I'm going to call those flaws "character." I want to appreciate the signs of a life well lived. The dirty shoes, fingerprints, stained clothing, and even the creepy-crawlies my kids sneak into the house. Those are all signs of life that I will look back on fondly. They bring memories and life-giving moments that a perfectly clean home never could.

I don't want to waste time on things that aren't important. I don't want to spend my time with my kids in guilt, wishing I could be better, when I could be using that time to just be with them and love them. I don't want to stare at myself in the mirror wishing I looked different when I could be using this body to move while it's still working. I don't want to spend my life worrying about what people think of me or wondering why they don't like me when I could be spending my time with family and people I love. I don't want to put my energy into working on how people perceive me. I don't want to spend my life trying to perfect it. I want to enjoy this life, whether people understand me or not. I want to spend my life *living*; I want to experience it.

I don't want to spend my life trying to perfect it.

I am not perfect at this imperfect living thing. There are times when life brings me trouble and I can feel myself falling back into my old ways. But when I do, I have a set of skills that helps me pull myself out of perfectionist thinking. With practice, I can recognize those thought patterns before I act on my perfectionism and shift my perspective back toward enjoying life.

This stuff takes practice. You can't just read something once and think it will magically erase all your perfectionist habits. Unraveling and releasing expectations takes work. If something in this book struck a chord with you, fold the top corner of the page so you can find it again. Write it down and reread it the next time you are struggling. Shifting your mindset won't happen overnight. It's a process I have been working through for years.

If you are open to the ideas in this book and repeat them to yourself enough, eventually you will memorize them. Over time, it will get easier and easier to trade perfectionism for a life full of peace and joy.

———————

You are not called to be perfect.

I hope you shift your perspective away from perfection and toward enjoying your life.

You don't need to be the best at anything.

I hope you let others win and stop comparing and competing with those around you.

You can't avoid criticism.

I hope you find the simplicity and freedom in letting other people misunderstand you.

You don't need to be like any other mom.

Different kids need different moms. All your kids need is for you to keep them safe, loved, and fed. I hope you love your people, and I hope you prioritize your experiences with them over appearances.

You don't need to spend any time making anything perfect.

Things will be okay if they are just good enough. I hope your house gets messy and you can appreciate the life within it.

There is no right way to get through your day.

I hope you fill your free time with things you love.

No accomplishment will prove your worth.

I hope you remember your value.

Making mistakes is an important part of life.

I hope you have the courage to make them.

I hope you prioritize memory making so that, when you are old, you have great moments to look back on.

I hope you focus on the small joys.

I hope you collect good things along the way.

I hope you grow around your grief.

I hope you find peace.

It takes courage to do what I'm suggesting; it isn't easy to change the way you've always done things. But it's worth it.

Go live your life. Enjoy it. Don't perfect it.

ACKNOWLEDGMENTS

I started taking notes on my phone over ten years ago. Those notes became the foundation of this book—a book that I was able to write because of the influence and support of others.

I want to start by thanking my husband, Jessie, the most supportive man in the world. Without him, I don't know where I would be, but I know my life would be a lot harder. Thank you for never hesitating to pick up the slack while I chase my dreams.

To my boys, thank you for being the best sons a mom could ask for and for teaching me about what really matters in life. I love you.

Lexi, I believe God strategically placed you in my life at the right time. There is nothing like having a friend, but especially a writing friend. You keep me motivated and make me a better version of myself.

Natalie Lakosil, my agent, thank you for believing in me. You understood my message, and you helped me make it clearer. You opened the door that made this book dream a reality. I can never thank you enough for your hard work and the support you have given me.

Rebekah Von Lintel, my editor, your positive feedback built my confidence as a writer. You helped me shape each page into exactly what I wanted it to be. Thank you for believing in this message. Kristin Adkinson, thank you for understanding what I meant, even when the words didn't make sense. Your editorial skills are exactly what this book needed.

I want to shout a giant THANK YOU to Brian Vos, Brianna DeWitt, Chris Kuhatschek, and everyone at Baker Books. You have been the greatest team to work with, and I am so grateful for my experience with you. Thank you for turning my words into a real, physical book.

To my teachers:

Dr. Douglas Gronburg, my Comp 1 teacher at Tulsa Community College, who asked if he could keep my paper to show as an example to his next class.

Mrs. Brenda Neal, my tenth-grade English teacher, who pulled me aside to compliment my poetry book.

Mrs. Cegielski, my seventh-grade social studies teacher, who gave me life lessons that taught me how to shift my perspective. I used those lessons a lot later in life.

I will never forget the way you three teachers made me feel. You led me here. Thank you.

And finally, to my mother, the woman who taught me how to persevere. She always told me I could do anything I set my mind to. You were right, Mom.

NOTES

Chapter 1 Perspective Changes Everything

1. Ashley Campbell, "Conquering Oral Aversions," *No Hands But Ours* blog, May 4, 2017, https://www.nohandsbutours.com/2017/05/04/conquering-oral-aversions/. Originally posted on *Under The Sycamore* blog.

Chapter 3 Don't Let Opinions Shape Your Life

1. Annie Dillard, *The Writing Life* (Harper & Row, 1981), 32, Kindle.

Chapter 6 You Can't Do It All, but You Can Enjoy What You Do

1. John Wooden, Success Presents Coach John Wooden Pyramid of Success, Motivational Quotes, accessed January 13, 2025, https://www.thewoodeneffect.com/motivational-quotes/.

Chapter 8 You Don't Have to Have It All Figured Out

1. Rainbow Rowell, *Attachments: A Novel* (Penguin, 2012), 185.

Chapter 9 Feel Your Sadness and Collect Your Good Things

1. Lois Tonkin, "Growing Around Grief—Another Way of Looking at Grief and Recovery," *Bereavement Care* 15, no. 1 (1996): 10, https://doi.org/10.1080/02682629608657376.

ELIZABETH DANKS ROBBINS
is a pediatric nurse and the
founder of Travel Grown.
Navigating motherhood as
a teen mom and high school
dropout, she graduated with
a bachelor's degree in nursing at age twenty-one. She
speaks and writes about anti-
perfectionism on Instagram
@CreekGrown, where she is
unafraid to be vulnerable and

share the embarrassing stuff that makes life real and relat-
able. She lives on a creek in Oklahoma, where she is raising
two sons with her husband.

Connect with Elizabeth:

CreekGrown.com

 @CreekGrown   @CreekGrown